Marriages

of

Goochland County, Virginia

1733-1815

Compiled by

KATHLEEN BOOTH WILLIAMS

CLEARFIELD

Reprinted for
Clearfield Company, Inc. by
Genealogical Publishing Co., Inc.
Baltimore, Maryland
1996, 1998, 2003

Originally published: Alexandria, Virginia, 1960
Reprinted: Genealogical Publishing Co., Inc.
Baltimore, 1979, 1986
© 1960 Kathleen Booth Williams
© transferred to Genealogical Publishing Co., Inc.
Baltimore, Maryland, 1978
All Rights Reserved
Library of Congress Catalogue Card Number 78-65700
International Standard Book Number 0-8063-0836-2
Made in the United States of America

In Memory of

ANNIE LEITCH DUNCAN
(Mrs. Charles Louis Booth)

My mother, who taught me the importance
of genealogy and instilled in me the love
of searching old records.

(She died May 28, 1949)

```
                              HENRICO
                               1634
                                 │
                                 │
                                 │
                                 │
                    Goochland ───┴────────────────┐
                      1728                         │
              ┌──────────┴────────┐                │
         Albemarle          Cumberland       Chesterfield
           1744                1749              1749
      ┌──────┴──────┐            │
   Amherst     Buckingham        │
    1761          1761           │
      │            │             │
      │        Fluvanna      Powhatan
      │          1777          1777
   Nelson         │
    1808          │
                  │
             Appomattox
                1845
```

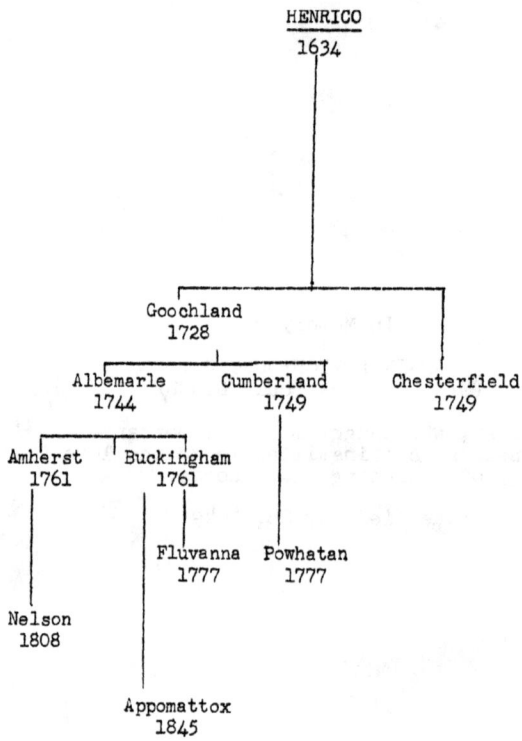

From:
Robinson's History of
Virginia Counties.
p. 166

FOREWORD

The General Assembly met on March 6, 1727. At this meeting an Act was passed for the division of Henrico County and the formation of Goochland County.

The full Act does not appear in Henning's Statutes but may be found in Robinson's History of Virginia Counties, p. 201. After the usual preliminaries it reads:
> That from and immediately after the
> First day of May next the said County of
> Henrico be divided into two distinct
> Counties ___ And that the division be
> made by a Line on the North side James
> River beginning at the mouth of Tuckahoe
> Creek thence up the said Creek to Chum-
> ley's Branch thence along a line of
> marked trees North Twenty degrees East to
> Hanover County And on the South side
> James River beginning at the Lower Mana-
> chin Creek from thence along a line of
> marked trees in a direct course to the
> mouth of Skinquarter Creek on Appomat-
> tox River And that that part of the
> County lying below the said line shall
> forever hereafter be called and known
> by the name of Henrico County And that
> that part of the County lying above the
> said line shall be called and known by
> the name of Goochland County And that
> all that part of the Parish of Henrico
> lying above the said line shall be in-
> cluded in and be part of the Parish of
> Saint James And that all of that part
> of the said Parish of Saint James lying
> below the said line shall be included
> in and be part of the Parish of Henrico
> any Act usage or Custom to the contrary
> thereof in any wise notwithstanding.

Goochland was named for William Gooch, Lieutenant-Governor of Virginia, 1727 - 1749*. (A Hornbook of Virginia History, p. 14).

When Goochland was formed it contained the area that is now Goochland, Albemarle, Cumberland, Amherst, Ches-

---

* The Encyclopedia Britannica, eleventh edition, Vol. XXVIII, p. 125, gives Governors of Virginia:
Under the Crown
William Gooch, Lieutenant Governor 1727-1740
Sir William Gooch, Governor 1741-1749.

terfield, Buckingham, Fluvanna, Powhatan, Nelson and
Appomattox. Albemarle was separated from Goochland
in 1744, (Henning V, 267): and Cumberland was separated from Goochland in 1748/9, (Robinson p. 78.
(See the Chart for subdivisions of Albemarle and Cumberland.

At a meeting of the General Assembly on September
18, 1744 an Act was passed for the Division of Saint
James Parish. It provided that that part of the Parish of Saint James, lying in Albemarle County, be
called and known by the name of Saint Anne's; the part
on the north side of James River, in the county of
Goochland, be called Saint James, Northam; the part of
the parish, lying south of the river to be known as
(Saint James) Southam. (Henning V, p. 267).

When Goochland was first formed Manakin Town also
was in its borders.

The Reverend William Douglas was one of the out-
standing ministers in Goochland County and the marriages he performed may be found in The Douglas Register.
I quote from the foreword:

> The Reverend William Douglas came to St.
> James Northam Parish, in Goochland
> County, Virginia, (Dover Church), on the
> 12th of October 1750. A memorandum in
> the Register shows that he had charge of
> St. James Northam Parish for twenty-seven
> years; Manakin Town (King William Parish)
> for nineteen years, and ministered to a
> charge in Buckingham County for four
> years.

The Reverend Mr. Douglas resigned from St. James
Northam Parish in 1777 and moved to Louisa County.

Other ministers performing marriages in Goochland between 1733 and 1715 were:

George Smith, Baptist	John James
Lewis Chaudoin	William Webber
Richard Pope	William Calhoon
Charles Hopkins	Richard Johnson
Reuben Ford	Dick W. Hallum
Samuel Woodfin	Conrad Speece
Leonard Page	W. Cooke
J. D. Logan	Charles Callaway
Hugh French	John W. Chaudoin
John D. Blair	Joseph D. Logan

These marriages were copied from the Marriage Register in the Virginia State Library, which Register was compiled from original records by the Virginia State Library Staff. Many of these marriages were found in Order Books and Deed Books and are so noted herein. One marriage, in this Register, was performed in 1730 and none was noted for 1731 or 1732. These bonds, along with others, have been lost.

Goochland is proud to have the bond for the marriage of Peter Jefferson to Jane Randolph. This bond has been repaired, framed and the frame is in a case hanging on the wall to the left as you enter the Clerk's Office.

I am deeply appreciative of the help and courtesy extended me by Mr. Harry W. Baldwin, Clerk of Goochland County.

                                    Kathleen Booth Williams

MARRIAGES OF GOOCHLAND COUNTY, VIRGINIA

1733 - 1815

5 December 1803. Dick ADAMS and Jane Banks, dau. of John Banks. Sur. Josiah Leake. Married 5 Dec. by Rev. Lewis Chaudoin. p 85

18 December 1798. James ADAMS and Jane Hodges. Sur. Thomas Hodges. Married by Rev. Lewis Chaudoin. p 68

20 April 1778. Robert ADAMS and Lucy Williams, dau. of Philip Williams. Sur. John Holland. Wit. Solomon Williams. Robert is son of James Adams of Albemarle County. John Graves makes affadavit that Robert is 21 years of age. p 20

23 December 1797. Thomas ADAMS and Martha Adams. Sur. James Adams. Wit. Richard Bates. Married 26 Dec. by Rev. Charles Hopkins. p 65

15 October 1798. Thomas ADAMS and Jane Ryan. Sur. Whitehead Ryan. Married 27 Oct. by Rev. Lewis Chaudoin. p 68

26 January 1796. William ADAMS and Nancy Higgason, dau. of Samuel Higgason. Sur. Nathan Crenshaw. Wit. James Adams. Married 28 Jan. by Rev. Charles Hopkins. p 59

17 October 1792. George ADDAMS and Aggey Harris. Sur. John Parrish. p 49

21 June 1784. William ADKINS and Winifred Clarke, dau. of Jeffry Clarke. Sur. James Shelton. Wit. Stephn Clarke and John Gill. p 29

27 June 1730. Giles ALLEGRE and Judith Cox. Sur. John James Flournoy. Wit. Henry Wood. p 1

5 December 1800. George ALLEN and Nancy Clements, dau. of Sally Clements. Sur. William Allen. Wit. Stephen Clements. Married 6 Dec. by Rev. Lewis Chaudoin. p 76

23 January 1799. James ALLEN and Nancy Alvis. Sur. John Riddle. Married 24 Jan. by Rev. Lewis Chaudoin who says Nancy _Avice_. p 69

19 October 1795. James ALLEN, Jr. and Tabitha Parrish, dau. of Moses Parrish. Sur. Fleming Payne. p 58

5 February 1795. William ALLEN and Lucy Graves, dau. of Lucy Graves. Sur. George Allen. Wit. Snead Graves. Married 7 Feb. by Rev. Hugh French. p 56

1 June 1798. John ALLHISON and Susanna Hodges. Sur.
Thomas Hodges, Jr. Married 2 June by Rev. Charles Hopkins.
p 66

12 November 1790. David ALVIS and Ann Comer. (Found in
Deed Book 15, p 452). Goochland Marriage Register p 396

2 November 1792. David ALVIS and Lucy Houchins, dau. of
Francis and Joice Houchins. Sur. William Groom. Wit.
John **Clement** and James **Clements**. Married 3 Nov. (Found in
Deed Book 16, p 147). Goochland Marriage Register p 49

15 October 1784. Elijah ALVIS and Elizabeth Clarke. Sur.
Shadrack Alvis. p 30

27 December 1784. Shadrack ALVIS and Judah Hancocke, dau.
of Major Hancocke. Sur. David Alvis. p 30

10 January 1800. Charles AMOS and Judith Profit. Sur.
David Glass. Wit. Richard Bates. Married 12 Jan. by
Rev. Richard Pope. p 74

24 January 1799. Francis AMOS and Nancy Profitt, dau. of
Sary Profitt. Sur. Jesse Profitt. Married 24 Jan. by
Rev. Dick W. Hallum. p 69

20 December 1802. Francis AMOS and Patsey Grubbs. Sur.
John Grubbs. Married 20 Dec. by Rev. Richard Pope. p 82

9 October 1811. Josiah AMOS and Patsy Alvis, dau. of
Judith Alvis. Sur. Francis Amos. Wit. Reuben Crenshaw.
Married 10 Oct. by Rev. Lewis Chaudoin. p 111

26 January 1769. Benjamin ANDERSON and Judith Mims, dau.
of David Mims, the elder. Sur. David Mims, Jr. p 13

1 January 1806. Benjamin ANDERSON and Rebecca Curd, dau.
of John Curd. Sur. Thomas Curd. Married 1 Jan. by Rev.
Charles Hopkins. p 92

30 November 1802. Edmund ANDERSON and Susanna Anderson,
dau. of Richard Anderson. Sur. Robert Perkins. Wit.
Elizabeth Snead. Married 2 Dec. by Rev. Charles Hopkins.
p 82

23 November 1809. Lawrence ANDERSON and Peggy Green, dau.
of John Green. Sur. William Moss. Married 23 Nov. by
Rev. Lewis Chaudoin. p 105

5 July 1796. Pouncey ANDERSON and Nancy Linch, dau. of
James Head Linch. Sur. Joseph Perkins, Jr. Wit. William L. Thompson. Married 7 July by Rev. Charles Hopkins. p 60

14 September 1786. William ANDERSON and Martha Hancock.
Married by Rev. Reuben Ford. (Deed Book 15, p 14). See
William Anderson. Goochland County Marriage Register
p 393

23 September 1786. William ANDERSON and Martha Hancock.
Sur. George Hancock. See William Anderson. p 34

14 January 1813. William ANDERSON and Mary G. Woodson,
dau. of John Woodson. Sur. Robert Perkins. Wit. J. R.
Woodson and Joseph Anderson. p 117

21 December 1807. David ARMSTRONG and Frances Mitchel
Pulliam, dau. of Zachariah Pulliam. Sur. J. Dickinson. p 99

3 January 1779. Daniel ASTON and Elizabeth McClain. Sur.
Joseph Watkins. p 22

4 November 1806. James ASTON and Martha Crenshaw, sister
of Reuben Crenshaw. Sur. Thomas Duke. Married 6 Nov. by
Rev. Charles Hopkins. p 95

31 August 1792. Isaiah ATKINSON and Lucy Ellis, (Henrico).
(Deed Book 16, p 130). Goochland County Marriage Register
p 397.

5 January 1796. Charles ATTKISSON and Mary Lewis. Sur.
John Lewis. Married 9 Jan. by Rev. Charles Hopkins. p 59

17 July 1787. James ATTKISSON and Betsy Saunders. Sur.
George Payne. p 37

27 August 1798. Joseph ATTKISSON and Marinda Shelton.
Sur. Thomas Shelton. Married 27 Aug. by Rev. Richard
Johnson who says Merenda. p 67

8 September 1806. William ATTKISSON and Frances Attkison, dau. of John Attkisson. Sur. Peter Attkison. Wit.
Thomas Loyd. p 94

28 December 1814. Tarlton BAGBY and Ann Cox. Sur. Trent
Cox. Married 29 Dec. by Rev. Lewis Chaudoin. p 123

6 March 1799. William BAGNALL and Tabitha Hopper. Sur.
Joshua Woodward. p 70

21 November 1791. John BAGWELL and Molly Michell. Sur.
George Holman. Married 24 Nov. (Deed Book 16, p 37 says
Milly Mitchell). Goochland County Marriage Register p 46

3 June 1761. Callam BAILEY and Betty Rowntree, dau. of
William Rowntree who is surety. p 9

9 December 1803. David BAILEY and Nancy Lacy, dau. of Susanna Lacy. Sur. Philip Lawson. p 85

1 October 1810. Julius BAILEY and Lucy Anderson. Meredith Anderson gives consent for Lucy. Sur. Allen Hunter. Julius Bailey is 21 years of age. p 108

1 September 1810. Julius BAILY and Lucy Anderson. Married by Rev. Lewis Chaudoin. See Julius Bailey. Goochland County Marriage Register p 317

12 January 1803. Peyton BAILEY and Nancy Sanders. Sur. William Sanders. Wit. Nicholas Vaughan. p 83

28 April 1813. William BAKER and Mary Moody. Clevears Baker is Mary's guardian. Sur. John M. Moody. Wit. Daniel Hooper. p 119

28 June 1770. Burgess BALL and Mary Chichester. John Payne gives consent for Mary. Sur. Archer Payne. Wit. Andrew Robertson and William Heale. Burgess Ball is of Lancaster County and James Ball is his guardian. p 15

11 December 1792. Leonard BALLEW and Sarah Wingfield, dau. of Fanny Wingfield. Sur. Jesse Wills. Wit. Mary Madox. Married 15 Dec. by Rev. William Webber who says Leonard Ballue and Sally Wingfield. (Order Book 19, p 328). Goochland County Marriage Register p 49

10 March 1813. Elisha BANKS and Nancy Lynch, Dau. of Polley Lynch. Sur. Robert Lynch. Wit. William Turner. "Both are people of color." Married 11 Mar. by Rev. Lewis Chaudoin. p 118

11 March 1812. Martin BANKS and Betsy Ann Howell, dau. of Charles Howell. Sur. William Howell. p 114

16 February 1808. William BANKS and Nancy Martin. Sur. John Martin. p 100

6 August 1766. George BARCLAY and Mary Cole, dau. of James Cole. Sur. William Thurston. p 11

19 May 1804. William BARKER and Elizabeth Crutchfield. Sur. Stapleton Crutchfield. Married 19 May by Rev. Lewis Chaudoin. p 87

13 July 1799. Hutchins BARNETT and Polley P. Matthews, dau. of Jean Barnett. Sur. Michael Robinson. Wit. John Barnett. Married 30 July by Rev. Richard Pope. p 71

30 April 1803. Jesse BARNETT and Sarah B. Matthews, dau.
of John and Jean Barnett. Sur. John Matthews. Wit.
Thomas Matthews. p 84

10 June 1779. Robert BARNETT and Elizabeth Farrar, 21
years of age, dau. of Thomas Farrar, deceased, and Elizabeth Farrar. Sur. Barrat Farrar. p 22

1 October 1806. John BARNFIELD and Patsey Holland. Sur.
Robert Parrish. p 95

19 December 1803. Abraham BASKETT and Frances Turner.
Sur. William Turner. p 86

31 January 1793. Arch^d BASS and Polly Hughes. (Order
Book 19, p 582). Goochland County Marriage Register p 399

10 August 1793. Jn° BASS and Ann Vaughan. Married by
Rev. Reuben Ford. (Order Book 19, p 582). See John
Bass. Goochland County Marriage Register p 398

22 August 1793. John BASS and Ann Vaughan. Sur. Matthew
Vaughan. Wit. Shadrack Vaughan. See John Bass. p 52

27 May 1806. Charles F. BATES and Mary Heath Miller.
Sur. Edward Trent. Wit. Samuel Branch. Married 28 May
by Rev. Reuben Ford who says Mary H. Miller. p 93

10 December 1810. William S. BATES and Huldah B. Parrish,
dau. of Booker Parrish. Sur. James Parrish. p 108

17 November 1788. Alexander BAUGH and Agnes Johnson, dau.
of Charles Johnson, Senr. Sur. Elisha Leake. Married 27
Nov. by Rev. William Webber. (Order Book 19, p 328).
Goochland County Marriage Register p 40

10 January 1786. Burrell BAUGH and Betsey Nevis, sis-
ter of John Nevis. Sur. George Payne. Married 19 Jan.
(Deed Book 15, p 480 says Burwell Baugh and Betsey Neaves.)
Goochland County Marriage Register p 33

18 September 1788. William BAUGH and Elizabeth Ashbrook,
of Chesterfield County. Married by Rev. George Smith,
Baptist. Goochland County Ministers' Returns p 313

11 July 1807. Bradley BELLAMY and Polly Parrish. Sur.
John T. Parrish. Married 14 July by Rev. Lewis Chaudoin.
p 97

18 January 1813. James BELLAMY and Precilla Bellamy, dau.
of William Bellamy. Sur. Bradley Bellamy. Wit. Charles
Faris and William Carven. Married 18 Jan. by Rev. Joseph
D. Logan who says Priscilla. p 118

11 June 1812. John BELLAMY and Milly Toler. Sur. Richard
Bellamy. Married 13 June by Rev. Lewis Chaudoin who says
Mildred. p 115

13 January 1813. Meredith BELLOMY and Elizabeth McBride,
(Betsey). Sur. John Fleming Parrish. Married 14 Jan. by
Rev. Lewis Chaudoin who says Meredith Bellamy and Eliza-
beth M. Bride. p 117

14 April 1815. Richard BELLAMY and Lucy Hodges. Sur.
James Hodges. Married 15 Apr. by Rev. Lewis Chaudoin.
p 124

10 July 1804. Stephen BENSON and Mourning Sadler. Sur.
Benjamin Sadler. Wit. Benjamin Anderson. Married 10
July by Rev. Charles Hopkins. p 88

16 July 1792. John BERNARD and Martha Norvell, dau. of
Thomas Norvell. Sur. Thomas Payne. Married 21 July.
(Deed Book 16, p 130). Goochland County Marriage Regis-
ter p 48

13 December 1787. Thomas BERNARD and Elizabeth Laprade,
dau. of John Laprade, deceased. Gideon Hatcher was exr.
for Susanna Laprade. Anderson Peers, exr., gives consent for Elizabeth. Sur. Tarlton Fleming. Wit. John
Matthews and John Crouch. p 38

28 December 1792. Thomas BERNARD and Mary Hicks, dau.
of Meshack Hicks. Sur. Joseph Mangam. Wit. Buckear
Carel and John Hicks. Married 29 Dec. (Deed Book 16,
p 147). Goochland County Marriage Register p 50

21 March 1748. William BERNARD and Mary Fleming. Sur.
Nicholas Davies. Wit. John Fleming, Jr. and H. Wood. p 4

12 May 1788. William BERNARD and Elizabeth Smith. Sur.
John Tate. Married 13 May by Rev. William Webber who
says William Barnard and Betsy Smith. (Order Book 19,
p 328). Goochland County Marriage Register p 39

30 June 1807. Alexander BERNLEY and Jonah Thurston,
dau. of Elizabeth Thurston. Sur. John W. Matthews.
Married 8 August by Rev. Lewis Chaudoin. p 97

9 October 1787. John BEVANS and Sicily Gilbert, granddaughter of Agnes Walker. Sur. Roland Blackburn. p 37

23 September 1815. Henry G. BIBB and Elizabeth Poor.
William M. Holman gives consent for both parties. Sur.
Charles M. May. Married 26 Sept. by Rev. Lewis
Chaudoin. p 125

3 May 1813. John BIGGAM and Jane Childress, of age, sister of Elijah Childress who is surety. p 119

5 June 1798. Thomas BINFORD and Susanna Jarratt. Sur. Robert Jarratt. p 67

24 September 1806. Thomas BINFORD and Magdalene Fowler. Married by Rev. Lewis Chaudoin. See Thomas Burford. Goochland County Ministers' Returns p 350

26 December 1805. William BISHOP and Cicily Moss. Samuel and Susanow Moss give consent for Cicily. Sur. William Moss. Wit. Lawrence Anderson. p 92

9 June 1814. John BLACK and Patsy Perkins. Sur. Anderson Bowles. p 121

7 December 1787. Reuben BLAKEY and Mary Royster. Sur. William Miller. p 38

10 June 1804. Ezekiah BLALOCK and Martha Utley, dau. of Obediah Utley. Sur. William Powell, Jr. p 87

12 December 1807. Francis BLANKENSHIP and Elizabeth Bowdry. Sur. David Glass. Married 24 Dec. by Rev. Lewis Chaudoin. p 99

22 November 1809. Francis BLANKENSHIP and Sally Daniel. Sur. William Ship. Married 1 December by Rev. Lewis Chaudoin. p 105

9 June 1787. Francis BLANKENSHIP and Polley Woolbanks, dau. of Salley Woolbanks. Sur. John Clements. Wit. George Drumwright and Thomas B___?___ . p 37

2 May 1785. Robert BLANKS and June Pleasants. Sur. Henry Gray. p 31

9 September 1808. John Curtis BLATCHFORD and Jane Rogers, of age. Sur. Joseph S. Ellis. p 101

21 January 1812. William BLUNKALL and Joanna Carrell, dau. of David Carrell. Sur. Robert A. McBride. Married 22 January by Rev. Lewis Chaudoin who says <u>Jane Carroll</u>. p 113

19 December 1808. Richard BOATWRIGHT and Jane Jarratt, dau. of Ann Jarratt. Sur. David Jarratt. Wit. Jo. Woodson. Married 22 Dec. by Rev. Lewis Chaudoin. p 102

2 November 1801. Archibald BOLLING and Catharine Payne, dau. of Archibald Payne. Sur. Archibald Payne, Jr. Married 5 Nov. by Rev. Charles Hopkins. p 79

14 February 1794. Edward BOLLING and Dorothea D. Payne, dau. of Arch. Payne. Sur. Jedediah Johnson. Married 17 Feb. by Rev. Charles Hopkins. (Order Book 19, p 582). Goochland County Marriage Register p 53

10 March 1800. Robert BOLLING and Jane Payne, dau. of Archer Payne. Sur. Archer Payne, Jr. Married 12 Mar. by Rev. Charles Hopkins. p 74

23 May 1796. William BOOKER and Sally Kelly. Sur. Thomas Woodson. Married by Rev. William Webber. p 60

27 July 1784. John BOUDRIE and Molly Layne. Sur. Henry M. Groom. p 29

26 October 1808. David BOURNE, Jr. and Elizabeth Jones, dau. of Landy Jones. Sur. John Richardson. Wit. George Bourne. p 101

23 December 1807. Arthur BOWLES and Elizabeth P. Cocke, dau. of James Cocke. Sur. John White. p 99

2 March 1797. Bartlett BOWLES, Jr. and Nancy Thomas, dau. of James Thomas. Sur. Richard Thomas. Married 2 Mar. by Rev. Lewis Chaudoin. p 62

24 May 1780. Charles BOWLES and Elizabeth Parrish, dau. of Joel Parrish. Sur. Matthew Lacy. Wit. David Hudson. p 24

14 November 1806. Charles K. BOWLES and Lucy P. Jackson, dau. of John Jackson. Sur. Thomas Bowles. Wit. Lucy White and Elisha Jackson. p 95

6 November 1804. Elisha BOWLES and Ann Mullins, niece of Conerley Mullins who states his brother, William, appointed Elisha Bowles executor in the presence of witnesses. Sur. Jesse Hodges. Married 8 Nov. by Rev. Lewis Chaudoin. p 88

4 June 1806. George BOWLES and Susanna Lovell. George Lovell gives consent for Susanna. Sur. Allen Parrish. p 93

12 November 1783. Hughes BOWLES and Mary Ship. Sur. Lewis Wilbourn. p 28

28 December 1813. Jacob BOWLES and Sophia Johnson. Sur. James Shelton. Married 28 Dec. by Rev. Lewis Chaudoin. p 120

16 December 1805. John BOWLES and Martha Cocke, dau. of James Cocke. Sur. Jack F. Cocke. p 92

27 November 1768. John BOWLES and Mary Redford, dau. of William Redford, deceased. Sur. John Cannon. Elizabeth Bowles makes affadavit that John, 21 years old last May, is son of Benjamin Bowles, deceased. p 13

20 August 1810. John BOWLES, Jr. and Susanna D. Ellis. Sur. John Smith Ellis. p 107

20 January 1812. Nathaniel V. BOWLES and Jane Puryear, dau. of Ann Puryear. Sur. Thomas H. Puryear. Wit. M. Smith. p 113

16 June 1806. Richard C. BOWLES and Elizabeth W. Pleasants, dau. of Philip Pleasants. Sur. Samuel Branch. p 93

13 March 1805. Seth BOWLES and Elizabeth Woolbanks, dau. of Sarah Woolbanks. Sur. William Drumwright. Wit. Samuel Branch. Married 21 Mar. by Rev. Lewis Chaudoin. p 90

2 October 1806. Thomas BOWLES and Elizabeth P. Bowles. Sur. John Bowles, Jr. p 95

14 February 1778. William BOWLES and Elizabeth Napier, dau. of Booth Napier. Sur. Martha Wood. Wit. Pete Walker, John Bowles, James Cawthorn and Charles Cawthorn. William is son of Deborah Bowles. p 20

25 December 1779. William BOWMAN and Mary Causby. Sur. Zachariah Haden. Wit. Ellison Clarke and Peter Clarke. William, 21 years of age on July 30, 1776, of Chesterfield County, is son of Joseph Bowman. p 23

28 April 1753. Benjamin BRADSHAW and Ann McBride, dau. of John McBride who is surety. Wit. Elizabeth McBride, David Murray and Aris Layne. p 6

27 September 1796. Benjamin BRADSHAW and Elizabeth Carter. Sur. William Carter. Married 29 Sept. by Rev. Lewis Chaudoin. p 61

21 December 1812. Benjamin BRADSHAW and Eliza S. Rutherford, dau. of Samuel Rutherford. Sur. William Turner. Wit. Will. Rutherford. Married 23 Dec. by Rev. Lewis Chaudoin who says Eliza S. Reatherford. p 116

15 December 1785. John BRADSHAW and Sally Johnson. Sur. Benjamin Sadler. John is son of Hannah Bradshaw. p 32

4 December 1781. Learner BRADSHAW and Ann Bradshaw. Sur. George Payne. p 26

8 December 1785. Robert BRADSHAW and Mary Bradshaw, dau. of Sarah Bradshaw. Sur. John Bradshaw. p 32

13 February 1790. William BRADSHAW and Mary Johnson. Sur. William Perkins. p 42

2 February 1799. John BRADY and Cynthia Pemberton. Sur. Micajah Parrish. Married 6 Feb. by Rev. Charles Hopkins. p 70

4 October 1804. Thomas BRANCH and Mrs. Sally Massie. Sur. George Layne. Wit. Dabney Parrish. Married 7 Oct. by Rev. Lewis Chaudoin. p 88

16 August 1810. Richard BRIDGWATER and Susanna E. Woodson. Stephen Woodson gives consent for Susanna. Sur. Thomas Woodson. p 107

27 November 1798. John BRITT and Elizabeth Cardin, "of lawful age." Sur. Joshua Houchins. Married 28 Nov. by Rev. Lewis Chaudoin who says Elizabeth <u>Carden</u>. p 68

20 September 1784. William BRITT, Jr. and Sarah Poor, dau. of Thomas Poor. Sur. Stephen Sampson. William Britt gives consent for William Britt, Jr. p 29

8 December 1802. William BRITT, Jr. and Patsey Mullins, dau. of Conaley Mullins. Sur. William Britt. Wit. John Mullins. Married 9 Dec. by Rev. Lewis Chaudoin. p 82

22 December 1815. Andrew BROADDUS and Jane C. Broaddus. Sur. Thomas Nelson. Wit. Eliza S. Broaddus. p 126

18 April 1797. John BROCKENBROUGH and Gabriella Randolph. Married by Rev. Charles Hopkins. Goochland County Ministers' Returns p 341

26 December 1807. William BROFFIT and Elizabeth Arne. Married by Rev. Leonard Page. See William Profit. Goochland County Ministers' Returns p 350

28 October 1790. John BROOKS and Nancy Atkison. Sarah Atkison gives consent for Nancy. Sur. A. Randolph. p 43

14 August 1813. Moses BROOKS and Betsy Howell, "one and twenty years of age," dau. of Patsy Howell. Sur. William Miller. Wit. William Archer and W. Brown. p 119

20 December 1813. Thomas BROOKS, Jr. and Nancy Blankenship. Sur. William Drumwright. Married 20 Dec. by Rev. Lewis Chaudoin. p 120

11 February 1810. Walker BROOKS and Sarah Sadler. Sur. Benjamin Sadler, Jr. and Austin Walker. Married by Rev. Leonard Page. Returned 18 Feb. 1810. p 106

29 February 1788. John BROWN and Jane Rowntree. Sur. Samuel Rowntree. p 39

6 February 1798. John BROWN and Tabitha Woodson, dau. of Elizabeth Woodson. Sur. William Miller. Married 9 Feb. by Rev. William Webber. p 66

9 October 1798. Joseph BROWN and Jane Blackwell. Sur. Jesse Blackwell. p 68

15 November 1788. Tarlton BROWN and Ann Fox. (Deed Book 15, p 240). See Tarlton Brown. Goochland County Marriage Register p 394

17 November 1788. Tarlton BROWN and Ann F. Napier. Sur. Jos. Payne. Wit. John Brown and Reubin I. Brown. See Tarlton Brown. p 40

28 December 1785. William BROWN and Isbell Herndon. Sur. Lewis Herndon. p 32

26 January 1811. Archibald BRYCE, Jr. and Mary B. Pemberton, dau. of Thomas Pemberton. Sur. Alexander S. Payne. Married 30 Jan. by Rev. J. D. Logan. p 109

8 June 1805. John BRYCE and Ann S. Gordon, niece of George Woodson Payne. Sur. Alexander S. Payne. p 90

1 May 1788. John BRYERS and Keturah Webber. Sur. Philip Webber. Married 1 May by Rev. William Webber who says John **Briers** and **Ketturah** Webber. (Order Book 19, p 328 also says John **Briers**). Goochland County Marriage Register p 39

21 January 1814. Pouncey BUNCH and Sally B. Mallory, 21 years of age. Sur. Fleming Massie. Married 26 Jan. by Rev. Lewis Chaudoin. p 121

2 January 1794. Littleberry BURCH and Jane Woodward. Reubin Branch makes affadavit that "Jane is 21 years of age this 2 Jan. 1794." Sur. Reuben Burch. Wit. Will Farrar. Married 3 Jan. by Rev. William Webber. p 53

17 January 1786. Nathaniel BURFORD and Mary Hodges. Sur. George Lovell. p 33

3 January 1799. Nathaniel BURFORD and Nancy Bowles. Sur. Bartlett Bowles. Married by Rev. Charles Hopkins. Returned 3 May 1799. p 69

10 September 1806. Thomas BURFORD and Magdaline Fowler, dau. of Alexander Fowler. Sur. Anselm Walker "or **Hanselm** Walker." See Thomas Binford. p 94

27 October 1790. James BURLEY and Mary Thurston. Sur. David Glass. Wit. William Allen. p 43

2 November 1763. Charles BURTON and Mary Holland, dau. of George Holland. Sur. George Holland and Michael Holland. Wit. John Miller and George West. Charles Burton was born in Jan. 1740, son of Robert Burton. Judith Payne, wife of George Payne, makes affadavit as to his age. p 11

16 March 1742. Hutchins BURTON and ___?___ ___?___ . , Sur. William Allin. p 2

17 March 1752. Robert BURTON and Sarah Jordan. Sur. Charles Jordan. Wit. Valentine Wood and Will Pryor. p 6

1 October 1757. Robert BURTON and Judith Laforce. Sur. John Smith. Wit. William Harding, William Stamps, William Burton and Francis Bickley. p 7

7 November 1815. Jacob BUSBY and Frances Glass, dau. of David Glass. Sur. Elisha Layne. Wit. James Busby. William Busby gives consent for Jacob. Married 9 Nov. by Rev. Lewis Chaudoin. p 126

25 December 1805. John BUSH and Polly Alvis, dau. of Shederick Alves. Sur. David Alvis, "of Elijah". p 92

10 December 1803. Caleb BUTLER and Jane Pace, 21 years of age. Sur. John Green. p 85

17 March 1800. Thomas BUTLER and Elizabeth Crutchfield. Sur. George Butler. p 74

17 October 1752. Joseph CABELL and Mary Hopkins. Sur. John Hopkins. Wit. William Cabell and William Cabell, Jr. Joseph is son of William Cabell. p 6

13 March 1800. Squire CAESAR and Rachel Cooper. Sur. Thomas F. Bates. Free negroes. Married 16 Mar. by Rev. Lewis Chaudoin who says, "each is a free negro" and spells the name Casar. p 74

2 December 1812. Alexander A. CAMMELL and Sarah Boyce. Married by Rev. Lewis Chaudoin. See Dr. Alexander A. Campbell. Goochland County Ministers' Returns p 353

26 November 1812. Dr. Alexander A. CAMPBELL and Sarah Boyce. George S. Smith gives consent for Sarah. Sur. Joseph A. Royster. Wit. John H. Royster. See Alexander A. Cammell. p 116

1 February 1793. Archer CARDEN and Molley Salmon, dau. of Benjamin Salmon. Sur. Jesse Carden. Married 2 Feb. (Deed Book 16, p 147). Goochland County Marriage Register p 51

28 July 1801. Jesse CARDEN and Clara Satterwhite. Sur. Samuel Nowell. Married 30 July by Rev. Charles Hopkins who says Clary. p 78

12 December 1815. David CARDIN and Sally Richards, of age, dau. of William Richards. Sur. James Halsey. Married 21 Dec. by Rev. Lewis Chaudoin. p 126

26 December 1791. Bucker CARRELL and Nancy Hicks. Meshack Hicks gives consent for Nancy. Sur. Jesse Witt. Married 29 Dec. (Deed Book 16, p 34 says Burker Carrell). Goochland County Marriage Register p 47

16 May 1791. Daniel CARRELL and Martha Allen. Sur. Stephen Sampson, Jr. Married 26 May. (Deed Book 16, p 37 says Daniell). Goochland County Marriage Register p 45

27 November 1787. David CARRELL and Salley Carrell, dau. of Roger Carrell. Sur. William Carrell. p 38

21 May 1803. Jesse CARRELL and Betsy East, dau. of Benjamin East. Sur. James Watkins. Married 30 May by Rev. Lewis Chaudoin. p 84

20 April 1799. Daniel CARTER and Sarah Dowdy, "of full age." Sur. Benjamin Phaup. Wit. Elizabeth Dowdy. p 71

17 October 1791. Martin CARTER and Nancy Page. Sur. William Page. Married 22 Oct. (Deed Book 16, p 34). Goochland County Marriage Register p 46

24 September 1809. Thomas CARTER and Peggy Rollins Taylor, dau. of John Taylor. Sur. William T. Taylor. Wit. John Taylor. p 105

3 March 1786. William CARTER and Nancy Attkisson, dau. of Henry Attkisson. Sur. Charles Attkisson. p 276

25 June 1802. William CARTER and Nancy Scott. Married by Rev. Leonard Page. Goochland County Ministers' Returns p 346

21 February 1815. William F. CARTER and Maria V. Woodson. Sur. Jacob Michaux. Wit. A. B. Baugh. Married 23 Feb. by Rev. Lewis Chaudoin. p 123

11 December 1805. Henry CARY and Elizabeth Morrissette, granddaughter of William Farrar. Sur. William Hix. Wit. Margaret Morrissette. Henry Cary is of Chesterfield County. p 91

19 September 1791. David CAUSBY and Susanna Whitt. Sur. Josiah Woodson. Wit. William Farrar. p 46

8 February 1760. Robert CAWTHON and _____ Leforce, dau. of Rene Leforce. Sur. Matthew Nightingale. Wit. Benjamin Hughes. See Robert Cothan. p 8

24 December 1789. Charles CAWTHORN and Elizabeth Williams. (Deed Book 15, p 478). Goochland County Marriage Register p 395

28 November 1794. Charles CAWTHORN and Mary Sanders, also written Mary Sandis on the bond, dau. of John Sanders. Sur. Shadrach Woodall. Wit. Joshua Woodward and Harry Gray. p 55

4 October 1807. John CHAMBERS and Elizabeth Wilmerton. Sur. Hill Winfrey. Married by Rev. Lewis Chaudoin. Returned 5 Dec. 1807. p 98

14 September 1791. John CHAMPION and Jane Depriest, dau. of Elizabeth Deprest. Sur. David Layne. Married 15 Sept. (Deed Book 16, p 34 says Dupriest.) Goochland County Marriage Register p 45

26 April 1784. Robert CHANCELLOR and Frances Christian, dau. of Andrew Christian. Sur. Thomas Chancellor. Wit. Jacob Christian. p 29

29 November 1786. Thomas CHANCELLOR and Milley Nowlin. Sur. Abraham Nowlin. Wit. William Miller. p 35

18 February 1746. Joseph CHATWIN and Fanny Bassett. Sur. Thomas Bassett. Joseph Chatwin is of Lancaster County. p 3

15 November 1784. Lewis CHAUDOIN and Kitty Mims. Sur. Gideon Mims. p 30

11 May 1813. Hezekiah CHEATHAM and Thursey Clarke, dau. of William Clarke. Sur. Thomas Green. Wit. Zacha R. Chittum. Hezekiah is son of John Chitham. Married 12 May by Rev. Lewis Chaudoin who says Thursa Clarke. p 119

30 October 1811. Ambler CHICK and Polly M. Ragland. Lewis Turner is Polly's guardian. Sur. Isham R. Woodson. Ambler Chick is 21 years of age. p 112

8 September 1806. Pettus W. CHICK and Elizabeth Turner,
dau. of Lewis Turner. Sur. William Cocke. Wit. Hardin
Turner. p 94

6 September 1805. John G. CHILDRESS and Margaret Faudree.
Sur. John S. Crutchfield. p 91

1 July 1809. Nelson CHILDRESS and Milly Attkisson, 21
years of age. Sur. Spotswood Childress. p 104

13 January 1814. Pendleton R. CHILDRESS and Maria Attkisson, dau. of Jonah Attkisson. Sur. John J. Childress.
p 121

17 December 1810. Spotswood CHILDRESS and Sally Johnson.
Sur. William Childress. Wit. Mard. Smith. p 108

30 May 1792. William CHILDRESS, Jr. and Rebecca Johnson.
Sur. Charles Cawthorn. Wit. Nicholas M. Vaughan. (Order
Book 19, p 328). Married 1 June by Rev. William Webber.
Goochland County Marriage Register p 48

14 March 1805. Thomas CHISHOLM and Elizabeth M. Gray,
dau. of Henry Gray. Sur. John Gray. Wit. David
Chisholm. Married 14 Mar. by Rev. Charles Hopkins. p 90

27 January 1800. Walter CHISHOLM and Elizabeth Pulliam,
dau. of Zachariah Pulliam. Sur. John Austin. Wit. John
L. Harris and Edm^d Underwood. p 74

31 December 1810. Cornelius D. CHISHOLME and Elizabeth
Swift. Each is "of full age". Sur. William H. Gray.
Wit. Thomas Swift and Maria Swift. p 109

22 October 1791. William CHITTAM and Nafanar Grubb.
Daniel Grubb gives consent for Nafanar. Sur. Jesse
Grubb. Married 23 Oct. (Deed Book 16, p 37). Gooch-
land County Marriage Register p 46

17 April 1815. Zachariah CHITTUM and Savara Green. Sur.
John Green. Married 20 Apr. by Rev. Lewis Chaudoin.
p 124

26 February 1811. John H. CHRISTIAN and Mary H. Bates.
Sur. William Miller. p 110

14 February 1805. Robert CHRISTIAN and Ann Mims. Sur.
Duguid Mims. Wit. Isaac Pleasants. Married 16 Feb. by
Rev. Lewis Chaudoin. p 90

3 January 1778. Turner CHRISTIAN and Anna Payne, dau. of
George Payne, Jr. Sur. William Gilliam. Wit. James
Gresham, Mary Gresham and Morning Christian. Turner is
son of Charles Christian. p 19

14 June 1798. Benjamin CLARKE and Agnes Tollor, dau. of
Susaner Tollor. Sur. Philip Lawson. p 67

8 September 1790. Elisha CLARKE and Elizabeth White. Sur.
John Gill. Wit. William Attkison and Clabourn Johnson.
Married 8 Sept. (Deed Book 15, p 487). Goochland County
Marriage Register p 42

24 June 1786. Isham CLARKE and Marian Fagg. Sur. William
Fagg. See Isham Clarke. p 33

25 June 1786. Isham CLARKE and Mary Ann Fagg. Married by
Rev. Reubin Ford. (Deed Book 15, p 14). Goochland County
Marriage Register p 393

19 May 1762. James CLARKE and Susanna Bibb, dau. of John
Bibb. Sur. William Bibb. Wit. John Bigger and John Bibb,
Junr. p 9

30 January 1787. Jesse CLARKE and Lucey Willis, dau. of
Ellender Willis. Sur. William Willis. Married 31 Jan.
by Rev. Reuben Ford. (Deed Book 15, p 14). Goochland
County Marriage Register p 36

16 October 1815. Richard CLARKE and Peggy Pryor, dau. of
S. Pryor. Sur. John W. Pryor. Married 18 Oct. by Rev.
Lewis Chaudoin. p 125

17 November 1789. Stephen CLARKE and Sally Crouch. Married 17 Nov. by Rev. William Webber. (Order Book 19, p
328). Goochland County Marriage Register p 395

19 June 1798. Turner CLARKE and Agnes Alvis. Sur. David
Alvis. Married 21 June by Rev. Lewis Chaudoin who says
Clark. p 67

18 March 1789. Turner CLARKE, Jr. and Elizabeth Ann Cragwall, (Betsy). Sur. Isham Clarke. p 41

21 April 1806. William CLARKE and Jane Jones. Sur. John
Layne. Married 8 May by Rev. Lewis Chaudoin. p 93

19 December 1814. William CLARKE and Elizabeth C. Jarratt,
dau. of Deux Jarrett. Sur. William Lewis. Married 24 Dec.
by Rev. Lewis Chaudoin. p 122

7 January 1811. William M. CLARKE and Peggy Meridith
Cocke. Sur. Samuel Cocke. William is son of Elisha
Clarke. Married 8 Jan. by Rev. Lewis Chaudoin who says
Peggey Meredith Cock. p 109

12 March 1761. William CLARKSON and Martha Pledge. William Pledge gives consent for Martha. Sur. William Rutherford. Wit. Jeremiah Rich, David Clarkson, Nathaniel Thompson and Thomas Jackson. William, 21 years of age, is son of Ansalm Clarkson. p 9

15 May 1815. Nathaniel H. CLAYBORNE and Elizabeth A. Binford, dau. of Thomas Binford. Sur. Jacob B. Fowler. Wit. Benjamin Anderson. Married 17 May by Rev. Lewis Chaudoin who says Claybourn. p 124

5 January 1795. Francis CLEMENTS and Phany Page, dau. of William Page, Sr. Sur. William Page, Jr. Married 6 Jan. by Rev. Lewis Chaudoin. p 56

19 January 1795. James CLEMENTS and Agnes Gilliam. Sur. Thomas F. Bates. Wit. Frederick Bates. Married 11 Feb. by Rev. Charles Hopkins. p 56

3 February 1786. Jesse CLEMENTS and Elizabeth Adams. Sur. Claburn Bradshaw. p 33

22 September 1779. Richard CLOUGH and Janey Woodson. Sur. Gideon Mims. Wit. George Clough, Jr. and Ro. Sydnor. Richard is son of George Clough who makes affadavit he is of age. p 23

20 December 1813. Woodson M. CLOUGH and Ann Lang. Sur. William Hodges. p 120

18 December 1799. Benjamin COCKE, Jr. and Betsy Nuckols, dau. of William Nuckols. Sur. John Lewis. Wit. Thomas Cocke. Benjamin is son of Benjamin Cocke, Sr. p 73

16 April 1800. David COCKE and Elizabeth Gilliam. John Gilliam gives consent for Elizabeth. Sur. William Cocke. p 75

19 October 1742. James COCKE, Junr and Mary Anne Chastain. Sur. Henry Wood. Wit. Joseph Dabbs and Isaac Bates. p 2

23 November 1774. James COCKE, Junr and Martha Holland Parrish, dau. of David Parrish who is surety. p 18

7 February 1807. Richard COCKE and Harriet Holland, dau. of Nathaniel Holland. Sur. John J. Dickenson. Wit. J. Hix. p 96

5 October 1802. Samuel COCKE and Susanna Woodson. Sur. William Johnson. p 81

13 August 1811. James COCKRAN and Elizabeth Wood, of age.
Sur. Joseph Scott, "James has resided on the plantation
of Jo. Woodson for 20 years." Married 15 Aug. by Rev.
Lewis Chaudoin. p 110

30 April 1790. John COCKRAN and Salley Johns. Jacob Banks
makes affadavit that Salley is "of lawful age." Sur. Reuben Turner. Married 2 May. (Deed Book 15, p 386.) Goochland County Marriage Register p 42

16 January 1797. Robert COLEMAN and Martha Lewis. Sur.
Stephen Crouch. Wit. William Lewis. Married 16 Jan. by
Rev. William Webber. p 62

25 December 1780. Samuel COLEMAN and Christian Forster.
Sur. William Lewis. p 25

5 February 1812. James COLLEY and Frances T. Williams,
dau. of Elizabeth Williams. Sur. John M. Williams. p 113

21 October 1788. Benjamin COLVARD and Mary George. Sur.
James George. p 40

16 December 1811. Jesse CONLEY and Martha Shepard, dau.
of James Shepard, Sr. Sur. Edward Matthews. Edward Matthews, Jr. makes affadavit that Jesse Conley "is fully 21
years of age." Married 17 Dec. by Rev. Lewis Chaudoin.
p 112

16 December 1803. Daniel COOPER and Nancy Cooper. James
Quigg makes affadavit that Nancy is a distance from her
parents. Sur. George Tyler. Married 17 Dec. by Rev.
Lewis Chaudoin. p 86

10 May 1799. Jacob COOPER and Aggy Guinn. Sur. Edward
Guinn. p 71

28 December 1812. Pleasant COOPER and Polly Hashaw, 21
years of age. Sur. Elisha Thacker. Wit. Thomas Miller,
Jr. p 117

13 December 1813. Randolph COOPER and Polly Cockran,
dau. of Henry Cockran. Sur. James Cockran. Wit. Jo.
Woodson. Married 16 Dec. by Rev. Lewis Chaudoin. p 120

31 October 1814. Roger COOPER, Jr. and Ruth Cockran,
dau. of Henry Cockran. Sur. Bartlett Horner. Wit. Jo.
Woodson. Married 3 Nov. by Rev. Lewis Chaudoin. p 122

7 September 1811. Samuel COOPER and Suckey Binns. Sur.
Benjamin Moss. Married 7 Sept. by Rev. Lewis Chaudoin.
p 111

29 August 1803. Wolloam COOPER and Nancy Banks, dau. of
Jacob Banks. Sur. Jacob Martin. William's name is also
written <u>William Cupper</u> on the bond. Married 1 September
by Rev. Lewis Chaudoin. p 84

24 December 1804. Parke CORNET and Nancy Demue, dau. of
Larose Demue. Sur. <u>Larrows Dimue</u>. Wit. John N. Haden.
p 89

24 September 1791. _____ COSBY and Susannah Witte. Married 24 Sept. by Rev. William Webber who says <u>David</u> Cosby
and <u>Susanna</u> Witte. (Order Book 19, p 328). Goochland
County Marriage Register p 396

17 September 1805. James M. COSBY and Nancy Layne. Sur.
William Layne. p 91

15 September 1788. Reuben COSBY and Lucy Alvis. Sur.
John Alvis. p 40

19 August 1767. Samuel COSBY and Mildred Poor, dau. of
Thomas Poor. Sur. Christopher Wood. Wit. Abraham Poor
and Janey Poor. p 12

14 January 1802. Thomas COSBY and Betsy Chancellor, for-
mer wife of David Chancellor. Thomas and Sarah Chancellor made affadavit that "their son, David, has been away
from his wife seven years and is married again." Sur.
Benjamin Phaup. p 80

31 October 1808. Zacheus COSBY and Nancy Richardson.
Sur. Robert Glenn. p 101

16 April 1801. Frank COUSINS and Chloe Cousins. Sur.
Edward Fuzmore. p 78

30 May 1812. Henry COUSINS and Lydia Pierce, 21 years
of age, dau. of John and Milly Pierce. Sur. Thomas Gilpin. E. Woodson makes affadavit that John Pierce is a
negro man of Dr. James Bryden's. Married 30 May by Rev.
Lewis Chaudoin. p 114

4 October 1811. William COUSINS and Polly Banks. Sur.
John Banks. Married 5 Oct. by Rev. Lewis Chaudoin. p 111

13 December 1794. Edward COX and Judith Humber. Sur.
John Humber. Married 18 Dec. by Rev. Charles Hopkins.
p 55

31 March 1794. Henry COX and Judith Eldridge, dau. of
Thomas Eldridge. Sur. Paul Dismukes. p 54

28 December 1811. Henry COX and Susan (Susannah) Jarratt, dau. of Ann Jarratt. Sur. James L. Browning. Wit. Richard Boatwright. Married 2 January 1812 by Rev. Lewis Chaudoin who says <u>Susanna</u>. p 113

21 October 1791. Jesse COX and Patsey Cooper, widow of Daniel Cooper. Sur. John Cox. Married 22 Oct. (Deed Book 16, p 37). Goochland County Marriage Register p 46

5 February 1810. John COX and Caty Brumfield, widow. Sur. Fleming Massie. Wit. Robert Meriwether. See John Cox. p 106

5 February 1810. John COX and Caty Brown. Married by Rev. Lewis Chaudoin. See John Cox. Ministers' Returns p 317

10 May 1796. Samuel N. CRAGWALL and Nancy Johnson, dau. of Jacob Johnson. Sur. Turner Clarke, Jr. Samuel's name is also written <u>Samuel N. Curwile</u> on the bond. Married 12 May by Rev. Charles Hopkins who says <u>Samuel N. Cragwall</u>. p 284

2 December 1812. Alexander A. CRAMMELL and Sarah Boyce. Married 2 Dec. by Rev. Lewis Chaudoin. Goochland County Ministers' Returns p 353

29 April 1805. Lipscomb CRANK and Polly M. Parish, dau. of Booker Parish. Sur. Stephen Crank. Wit. George W. <u>Parrish</u>. p 90

22 March 1808. Stephen CRANK and Mary A. Chisholm, dau. of Thomas Chisholm. Sur. Anderson Hopkins. Wit. Nelson Hopkins. p 100

21 December 1792. William CRANK and Elizabeth Hall, dau. of Jane Hall. Sur. Thomas Green. p 50

23 June 1806. Byars CRAWFORD and Martha Watkins. Ben Watkins gives consent for Martha. Sur. Milner Woodson. p 94

31 March 1810. Asbury CRENSHAW and Ann Coleman Pemberton, dau. of Thomas Pemberton. Sur. Preston Smith. Married 4 April by Rev. Conrad Speece. p 107

16 January 1809. John CRENSHAW and Polly Owen, dau. of William Owen. Sur. David A. Owen. Married 19 Jan. by Rev. Lewis Chaudoin. p 103

13 September 1808. George CREWDSON and Frances Walker. Sur. Shadrack Walker. p 101

20 October 1787. John CROUCH and Lucy Farrar of Powhatan
County. Married by Rev. George Smith, Baptist. The bond
for this marriage is in the Powhatan County Marriage Register and the above record in Goochland County Ministers'
Returns. p 313

5 November 1812. Richard CROUCH and Martha Britt, dau.
of William Britt, Sr. Sur. James Hopkins. Wit. Bolling
Britt. Married 10 Dec. by Rev. Lewis Chaudoin. p 116

16 April 1787. Stephen CROUCH and Marget Boles. Sur.
William Blunkall. Wit. John Hogan and Stephen Crouch,
Jr. Married 19 April. (Deed Book 15, p 15 says Marget
Bowles.). Goochland County Marriage Register p 36

24 November 1789. William CROUCH and Sally Downs Radford. (Deed Book 15, p 478). Goochland County Marriage
Register p 395

11 July 1801. John S. CRUTCHFIELD and Jane Faudree.
Sur. Nicholas Crutchfield. p 78

11 August 1786. Nicholas CRUTCHFIELD and Sarah Williams.
Sur. Charles Nuckles. See Richard Crutchfield. p 34

31 August 1786. Richard CRUTCHFIELD and Sarah Williams.
Married by Rev. Reuben Ford. (Deed Book 15, p 14.).
See Nicholas Crutchfield. Goochland County Marriage
Register p 393

6 June 1798. Robert CRUTCHFIELD and Polly Nuckols, dau.
of Samuel Nuckols. Sur. Nicholas Crutchfield. Married
3 June by Rev. Reuben Ford. p 67

17 August 1789. Stapleton CRUTCHFIELD and Nancy Layne.
Sur. Anthony Layne. p 41

20 June 1808. Stapleton CRUTCHFIELD and Jinny Sladyon.
Sur. William D. Slaydon. Married 25 June by Rev. Lewis
Chaudoin who says Staypleton Crutchfield and Jenny
Slaydyon. p 100

20 December 1808. Isaac CURD and Jane Watkins. Sur.
William Miller. p 103

10 July 1787. John CURD and Nanny W. Curd. Sur. Edmund Curd. Married 10 July by Rev. Reuben Ford. (Deed
Book 15, p 14). Goochland County Marriage Register p 37

25 March 1789. Newton CURD and Ann Elizabeth Hatcher,
dau. of Thomas Hatcher. Sur. Edmund Curd. Wit. Sarah
Hatcher. p 41

28 October 1815. Thomas CURD and Caroline R. Pleasants.
Sur. William Miller. Married 31 Oct. by Rev. J. D. Logan.
p 126

17 May 1783. John CURLE and Elizabeth Rowntree. Sur.
Randal Rowntree. p 28

1 July 1733. Joseph DABBS and Nancy (torn out)gatt. Sur.
Anthony Hoggatt. p 1

15 June 1786. Gwathney DABNEY and Elizabeth Maddocks, dau.
of James Maddocks. Sur. Tarlton Payne. Wit. Thomas Payne
and William George. p 33

9 June 1812. Robert DABNEY and Febus Mosley, dau. of
Kerz. Mosley. Sur. Thomas W. Pulliam. p 115

24 December 1807. Alexander Spotswood DANDRIDGE and Jane
Lewis. Married by Rev. Conrad Speece. Goochland County
Ministers' Returns p 350

10 September 1798. Archibald B. DANDRIDGE and Elizabeth
M. Underwood, dau. of George Underwood. Sur. Francis
Underwood, Jr. Wit. George Underwood, Jr. Married 13
Sept. by Rev. Charles Hopkins. p 67

23 November 1810. John B. DANDRIDGE and Mary Underwood.
Sur. Thompson W. Pulliam. Wit. George W. Watkins. p 108

2 August 1779. Nathaniel West DANDRIDGE, Senr and Jane
Pollard. Sur. Joseph Pollard, Sr. Wit. James Meri-
wether, John Curd and Joseph Pollard, Jr. Nathaniel West
Dandridge, Senr is of Hanover County. p 23

6 December 1808. Robert H. DANDRIDGE and Elizabeth T.
Dandridge, dau. of Mildred Dandridge. Sur. Arch^d B.
Dandridge. Wit. Robert A. Dandridge. p 102

16 January 1810. Watson DANDRIDGE and Eliza Moore, dau.
of John S. Moore. Sur. Arch^d B. Dandridge, (Is this a
double wedding? See William Fontaine.). p 106

25 June 1800. William S. DANDRIDGE and Nancy Harris Pul-
liam, dau. of William Pulliam. Sur. Robert J. Pulliam.
Wit. Arch^d B. Dandridge. Married 26 June by Rev. Charles
Hopkins. p 75

19 September 1805. Gerret DANIEL and Nancy Comer. Sur.
Obadiah Daniel. Gerret is son of John Daniel. p 91

23 January 1781. James DAVENPORT and Mary Rutherford,
dau. of William Rutherford who is surety. James Davenport is of Spotsylvania County. p 25

9 April 1793. John DAVENPORT and Nancy Willis, dau. of
Salley Willis. Sur. Philip A. Rice. Wit. Molley Redd,
Benjamin Davenport and Bartlett Willis. John is son of
Benjamin Davenport. Married 20 April by Rev. William
Webber. (Order Book 19, p 328). Goochland County Mar-
riage Register   p 51

20 April 1812. Tarlton DAVENPORT and Susan A. Parrish,
dau. of David M. Parrish. Sur. Sherwood Parrish. p 114

22 June 1813. Nathaniel DAVIDSON and Polly Redd, dau. of
Jesse Redd. Sur. Frances W. Redford. p 119

19 December 1733. Nicholas DAVIES and Judith Randolph.
Sur. Middleton Shaw. p 1

9 March 1812. Chisholm DAVIS and Dosha Austin, dau. of
John Austin. Sur. Fleming Austin. Wit. Larkin A.
Davis. p 114

11 October 1812. George DAVIS and Anney Turner, dau. of
William Turner. Sur. Pleasant Turner. p 115

17 August 1786. Henry W. DAVIS and Judith Walmack. Sur.
David Lanior. Wit. David Layne and Thomas Payne. p 34

20 March 1780. John DAVIS and Nancy Hall, dau. of Janie
Hall. Sur. David Layne. Wit. Reubin Weatherspon. John
Davis , "consent only". p 24

25 October 1785. John DAVIS and Nancy Walmack, dau. of
Richard Walmack, who is surety. Also, his name is
spelled Richard Wamack on the bond. p 31

20 March 1790. John DAVIS and Ann Hall. No surety is
given. Married 20 March. (Deed Book 15, p 385).
Goochland County Marriage Register p 42

12 June 1811. John S. DAVIS and Jane W. Matthews, dau.
of John and Jane Barett. Sur. John W. Matthews. Wit.
Polley Mathews. Married 17 June by Rev. Lewis Chaudoin.
p 110

13 May 1811. Thomas DAVIS and Polly Mitchell, dau. of
David Mitchell. Sur. John Mitchell. Wit. Finch Ragland, John S. Davis and John D. Mitchell. p 110

20 November 1753. Joseph DAWSON and Judith Dudley. Sur.
James George. Wit. David Murray. p 6

28 December 1815. Elijah DAY and Judith Banks, 21 years
of age, dau. of John Banks. Sur. Jacob Martin. p 127

9 January 1782. John DENNIS and Sarah Roundtree, dau.of Randol Roundtree. Sur. Robert Wade. p 26

22 June 1814. David DENTON and Nancy J. Duke. Sur. Edmund Duke. Married 23 June by Rev. Lewis Chaudoin who says Mary Johnson Duke. p 122

25 January 1814. James DENTON and Ann Perkins. Sur. Joseph Perkins. Wit. George W. Watkins. p 121

27 December 1802. John DENTON and Sally Cogil. Sur. John Cogil. Married 27 January 1803 by Rev. Lewis Chaudoin. p 83

20 February 1810. William DENTON and Sally Redd, 21 years of age, dau. of Mary Redd. Sur. George Barnett. Wit. Lucy W. Redd. P 106

2 December 1782. John DEPP and Elizabeth Perkins. Sur. Constant Perkins. p 27

19 December 1805. William DICKERSON and Unity Duke, dau. of Sary Duke. Sur. Cosby Duke. p 92

7 December 1807. Jonathan DICKINSON and Polly A. Dabney. Sur. William Johnson. p 98

17 September 1804. William DICKSON and Polly Helms, dau. of Sarah Helms. Sur. Micajah Parrish. William's name is also written William Dixon on the bond. Married 17 Sept. by Rev. Lewis Chaudoin. p 88

3 January 1800. Larrows DIMUE and Mrs. Betsey Williams. Sur. William Turner. Married 3 Jan. by Rev. Richard Pope. p 74

26 November 1788. Paul DISMUKES and Sally Richardson, dau. of George Richardson. Sur. George Payne. p 40

24 November 1745. William DIUGUID and Ann Morse, dau. of Alexander Moss. Sur. Constant Perkins. Wit. James Meredith, Frans Amoss and John Binns. p 3

22 February 1799. Benjamin DOWDY and Sally Smith, dau. of George Smith. Sur. George S. Smith. Married 23 Feb. by Rev. Charles Hopkins. p 70

25 July 1794. William DOWNER and Polly Woodson. Sur. Richard Redford. Wit. Carter Marshall. Married by Rev. Charles Hopkins. p 54

8 March 1793. Bennett DRUMRIGHT and Elizabeth Crafton. Married by Rev. Lewis Chaudoin. (Order Book 19, pp 440, 441). Goochland County Marriage Register p 398

15 October 1792. Bennett DRUMWRIGHT and Elizabeth Crafton, dau. of Polly Crafton. Sur. Harrod Pruitt. See Bennett Drumright. p 49

8 July 1786. George DRUMWRIGHT and Elizabeth Riddle. Sur. Archibald Riddle. Wit. Archer Riddle. p 34

14 February 1805. John DRUMWRIGHT and Polly Scott. Sur. John Lane (or Layne). Wit. Washington Drumwright and Dabney H. Jones. Married 16 Feb. by Rev. Lewis Chaudoin. p 90

6 June 1804. Thomas DUDLEY and Ann Underwood. Sur. Archibald B. Dandridge. Wit. John B. Dandridge. Married 9 June by Rev. Charles Hopkins. p 87

9 November 1784. George DUIGUID and Nancy Sampson. Sur. William Poor. p 30

31 August 1814. Benjamin B. DUKE and Mary Winston. John Shelton is Mary's guardian. Sur. Charles Attkisson. p 122

26 May 1769. Edmund DUKE and Jane Gresham, dau. of James and Elizabeth Gresham. Sur. Robert Coleman. Wit. William Gresham and James Gresham, Jr. Charles Christian, Jr. is guardian of Edmund Duke. p 14

30 January 1809. Edmund DUKE and Milley Demure, dau. of Lawrous Demure. Sur. Fontain Duke. p 103

6 June 1808. Fountaine DUKE and Judith N. Pryor, of age, dau. of William Pryor. Sur. Robert Meriwether. Married 6 June by Rev. Leonard Page. p 100

1 July 1805. George DUKE and Nancy Crenshaw, dau. of Benjamin Crenshaw. Sur. Philip P. Winn. Wit. Thomas Crenshaw. p 90

25 August 1798. Daniel DUNNAVANT and Polly Gennatt, dau. of Thomas Gennatt. Sur. Thomas Dunnavant. Married 28 Aug. by Rev. Richard Pope. p 67

21 March 1798. Thomas DUNNAVANT and Betsy Thurston. Sur. William Thurston. Wit. Richard Bates. Married 24 Mar. by Rev. Richard Pope. p 66

29 December 1812. Robert K. DUVALL and Elizabeth Turpin. "Both are of lawful age". Sur. John Satterwhite. Married 30 Dec. by Rev. Lewis Chaudoin who says Robert R. Duvall. p 117

15 July 1796. William Gray DUZAN and Patsey Carter, dau. of Richard Anderson. Sur. William Fuqua. Wit. John Woodson and Robert Perkins. Married 18 July by Rev. Lewis Chaudoin. p 60

7 October 1812. Samuel DYER, Jr. and Martha T. Watkins. Benjamin Watkins is Martha's guardian. Sur. Isaac Curd. Wit. John Trevilian. p 115

30 December 1795. Thomas EAGAN and Mildred Parrish. Sher^d Parrish gives consent for Mildred. Sur. William Parrish. Married 31 Dec. by Rev. Charles Hopkins. p 59

23 December 1745. Robert EASLY and Hannah Bates, dau. of Susanna Woodson. Sur. Rodrick Easly. Wit. James Bates. p 3

5 September 1772. Augustine EASTIN and Mary Ford, dau. of Thomas Ford. Sur. Hugh Moss. Wit. Macajah Clark and Christopher Clark. Augustine, 21 years of age the 9th of Sept. 1772, is son of Thomas Eastin of Albemarle County. p 16

5 January 1775. Thomas Baley EDDES and Elizabeth Rutherford, dau. of William Rutherford who is surety. Wit. Samuel Pryor. p 18

3 October 1807. Thomas EDDS and Catharine A. Parrish. Married by Rev. John James. (2 entries). See Thomas Edds. Goochland County Ministers' Returns p 315

30 October 1807. Thomas EDDS and Catherine A. Parrish. Sur. John Smith. See Thomas Edds. p 98

21 August 1786. Robert EDWARDS and Sarah Jordan. Sur. Elliott Lacy. Wit. William Miller. p 34

17 September 1810. Robert EDWARDS and Mourning Blalock. Sur. Hezekiah Blalock. p 108

11 March 1801. William EDWARDS and Patsy Jordan, dau. of Elizabeth Blalock. Sur. James Edwards. p 78

3 August 1807. John R. B. ELDRIDGE and Susanna Miller. Sur. Ro. Haden. Married 5 Oct. by Rev. Lewis Chaudoin. p 97

30 May 1802. William ELLIOTT and Ann East, dau. of Ann Hyde and step-daughter of Robert Hyde. Sur. Rice Graves. p 81

3 January 1801. Peter ELLIOTTE and Rebecca Morton, of age, dau. of Ann Morton. Sur. Rice Graves. Wit. Andrew McKim, Alex^r McKim and Robert McKim. p 77

24 November 1815. Absolam ELLIS and Polly Powell. dau. of William Powell, Senr. Sur. Joseph D. Watkins or Peter Watkins. p 126

29 October 1800. Andrew ELLIS and Judith Carden, dau. of
Robert Carden. Sur. William Williams. Married 30 Oct.
by Rev. Richard Pope. p 76

15 August 1796. Caleb ELLIS and Sally McCaul. Sur.
Stokes McCaul. Married 15 Aug. by Rev. William Webber.
p 61

13 December 1792. Charles ELLIS and Nancey Ellis (Henrico). (Deed Book 16, p 130). Goochland County Marriage Register p 398

16 December 1801. Eleazer ELLIS and Jane Nuckols. Sur.
Benjamin Cocke, Jr. p 79

23 August 1792. Henry ELLIS and Lucy Ford. Elizabeth
Ford gives consent for Lucy. Sur. Isaiah Attkisson.
Wit. Stephen Ellis and Charles Ellis. Married 31 Aug.
by Rev. William Webber. (Order Book 19, p 328). Goochland County Marriage Register p 48

15 February 1790. Humphray ELLIS and Susanna Holland.
Sur. George Payne. p 42

18 January 1802. James A. ELLIS and Martha Rowntree.
Sur. Samuel Rowntree. Wit. D. Guerrant and Harris Ellis.
James is son of David Ellis of Henrico County. p 80

9 March 1763. Jesse ELLIS and Sarah Woodson, dau. of
Joseph Woodson. Sur. John Crouch. Wit. Robert Shep-
ard, Robert Woodson, William Hodges, David Maddox and
Robert Huddeston. Jesse is son of Thomas Ellis. p 10

1 October 1787. John ELLIS and Mary Redford, dau. of
Edward Redford. Sur. Richard Redford. p 37

11 October 1784. Rice ENNES and Frances Mullins. Sur.
Jesse Mullins. p 30

18 July 1791. Archer EVANS and Jane Wade, dau. of
Robert Wade. Sur. William Rowntree. Wit. Thomas
Rowntree. Married 28 July by Rev. William Webber.
(Order Book 19, p 328). Goochland County Marriage
Register p 45

1 August 1795. John FARMER and Rebecca Askew. Sur.
Thomas Farmer. Married 1 Aug. by Rev. Lewis Chaudoin
who says Rebekah Asque. (Is this a double wedding?
See Thomas Murrer). p 57

18 April 1791. Robin FARMER and Frankey Green. Sur.
William Green. Married 25 April. (Deed Book 16, p 38
says Robert Farmer and Frances Green). Goochland County
Marriage Register p 45

20 June 1794. Thomas FARMER, Jr. and Lucy Green. Sur.
John Green. Married 20 June by Rev. Lewis Chaudoin. p 54

4 December 1805. John FARR and Lucy Parrish, dau. of
Aaron Parrish who is surety. p 91

15 March 1779. Barrott FARRAR and Sarah Harris, Sur.
Stephen Crouch. Wit. Joseph Farrar. p 22

10 March 1784. Benjamin FARRAR and Eliza. Cockrane. Sur.
Mary Cockrane. Wit. Fleming Payne. p 29

2 December 1801. Drury FARRAR and Elizabeth Banks, dau.
of Jacob Banks. Sur. John Tyler. Married 3 Dec. by Rev.
Lewis Chaudoin. p 79

27 December 1781. John FARRAR and Sarah Harris. Sur.
Barrett Farrar. p 26

1 February 1778. Joseph FARRAR and Sarah Farrar, dau. of
John Farrar. Sur. Stephen Crouch. Wit. John Hamner and
Thomas Farrar. p 20

17 December 1782. Matthew FARRAR and Martha Murrel. Sur.
Drury Murrell. p 27

19 August 1782. Robert FARRAR and Fanny Woodson. Sur.
Matthew Woodson. p 27

12 November 1808. Royall FARRAR and Margarett Morrissette,
(Margrete), granddaughter of William Farrar. Sur. William
Hix. p 102

29 May 1800. Thomas B. FARRAR and Patsy Moore, dau. of
Amos L^d. Moore. Sur. Joshua Woodward. p 75

16 March 1762. William FARRAR and Elizabeth Bibb, "under
21 years of age", dau. of John Bibb. Sur. Joseph Woodson.
Wit. William Bibb and John Bibb, Jr. p 9

23 November 1796. William FARRAR, Jr. and Mary Bernard,
of lawful age, dau. of Joshua Bernard. Sur. Reuben Ford,
Jr. Wit. John Bernard. p 61

16 October 1815. John W. FAUDREE and Elizabeth B. Ford.
Sur. Thomas Lynch. p 125

7 January 1802. Major FAUDREE and Patsey Attkisson, dau.
of Judah Attkisson. Sur. Elisha Barnett. Wit. Robert
Powers and Joseph Faudree. p 80

15 December 1783. Vachel FAUDRIE and Mary Gordon. Sur.
John Gordon. p 28

10 November 1790. Thomas FAUGHDREW and Polly Atkins, dau. of Judah Atkins. Sur. R. B. Payne. Wit. Stephen Southworth and Joseph Faudree. (In the Marriage Register and written in pencil above Polly's name is 'Atkisson'). p 43

1 May 1778. James FERGUSON and Judith Price, widow of Leonard Price, deceased. Sur. Lucy Wood. p 20

7 June 1805. James B. FERGUSON and Jane S. Bolling, widow of Robert Bolling. Sur. Archer Payne, Jr. Wit. Judith S. Hylton. p 90

15 August 1808. James B. FERGUSON and Sally Gay, dau. of William Gay. Sur. John Smith. Wit. Francis Thornton and Thomas B. Gay. Married 18 Aug. by Rev. Conrad Speece. p 101

25 October 1770. Benjamin FITZPATRICK and Mary Perkins, dau. of Mary Perkins. Sur. Joseph Fitzpatrick, of Albemarle County. Wit. Constant Perkins and Judah Perkins. Benjamin is of Albemarle County. p 15

26 March 1791. Thomas M. FLEMING and Nancy Payne. Sur. William Miller. Married 1 April. (Deed Book 15, p 487). Goochland County Marriage Register p 44

16 December 1793. William R. FLEMING and Nancy Webb. Sur. George Webb. p 53

13 December 1813. Gideon FLIPPO and Sally Woodson. Samuel Woodson is her brother and guardian. Sur. Philip Woodson, Jr. Married 21 Dec. by Rev. Lewis Chaudoin who says Flippoe. p 120

21 July 1801. John FLOURNOY and Sally Ford, dau. of William Farrar. Sur. William Farrar, Jr. p 78

24 December 1787. John F. FLOURNOY and Mary Ashurst, of Chesterfield County. Married by Rev. George Smith, Baptist. Goochland County Ministers' Returns p 313

2 April 1748. Samuel FLOURNOY and Elizabeth Harris, dau. of John Harris. Sur. Henry Wood. Wit. James Harris and William Harris. p 4

21 November 1785. Baxter FOLKES and Susanna Weber. Sur. Philip Weber. Married 8 Dec. (Deed Book 15, p 408 says Baxter Folks and Susanna Webber). Goochland County Marriage Register p 32

16 January 1810. William FONTAINE and Martha Hale Dandridge, dau. of N. W. Dandridge. Sur. Archd B. Dandridge. Wit. Claiborne Mallory, William Pulliam and Nimrod Chisholm. (Is this a double wedding? See Watson Dandridge.) p 106

23 December 1799. John FORBES and Elizabeth Bryce, dau. of Arch^d. Bryce. Sur. James F. Leitch. Married 24 Dec. by Rev. Charles Hopkins. p 73

13 November 1799. John FORD and Nancy Hughes. Sur. Ellis Puryear. p 72

14 May 1792. Reuben FORD, Jr. and Sally Farrar, dau. of William Farrar. Sur. John Brown. Wit. Ro. Farrar and Jesse Payne. Reuben is son of Reuben Ford. Married 15 May by Rev. Reuben Ford. (Order Book 19, p 327). Goochland County Marriage Register p 48

6 July 1793. Timothy FORD and Betsy Webber, dau. of William Webber. Sur. James Carter. Wit. Mary Ford, Reuben Ford, Jr., John Webber and Sally Webber. Timothy is son of Reuben Ford. p 51

16 February 1807. William A. FORD and Mary Heath Miller. Sur. Paul Dismukes. p 97

4 September 1789. John FORLINES and Susanna Poor. (Deed Book 15, p 386). Goochland County Marriage Register p 394

14 April 1780. Alexander FOWLER, Jr. and __?__ Smith, dau. of George Smith who is surety. Wit. Sherwood Fowler. John Shelton makes affadavit that Alexander, son of Alexander Fowler, Sr., is over 21 years of age. p 24

5 February 1805. Jacob FOWLER and Nancy Ware, dau. of James Ware. Sur. William Holman. Married 7 Feb. by Rev. Lewis Chaudoin. p 89

18 December 1809. William FOWLER, Jr. and Mary Salmons. Sur. John Philpotts, Jr. Married 21 Dec. by Rev. Lewis Chaudoin. p 105

10 September 1791. Donald FRASER and Mary Crowdas. Sur. William Allen. Married 24 Sept. (Deed Book 16, p 38). Goochland County Marriage Register p 45

19 September 1800. Orange FREEMAN and Patsy Scott. Sur. Riley Scott. Married 20 Sept. by Rev. Lewis Chaudoin. p 75

24 September 1806. Thomas FREEMAN and Martha Bailey, dau. of Callam Bailey. Sur. John G. Bailey. Wit. Richard Layne and Callom H. Bailey. Married 25 Sept. by Rev. Lewis Chaudoin. p 95

29 July 1795. Titus FREEMAN and Molley, "a free woman". Sur. _____. Married 17 Aug. by Rev. Lewis Chaudoin. p 57

20 May 1805. Wyatt FREEMAN and Elizabeth O. Clements.
Sur. Benjamin Bradshaw. Married 22 May by Rev. Lewis
Chaudoin. p 90

4 January 1813. Wyatt FREEMAN and Jane Gray. Henry Gray
gives consent for Jane. Sur. Rowland Hopkins. Married 6
Jan. by Rev. Lewis Chaudoin who says Jane M. Gray. p 117

3 September 1804. Mason FRENCH and Nancy Perkins. Sur.
Archelaus Perkins. Wit. Benjamin Anderson. p 88

28 February 1801. Robert FRENCH and Molley Hopkins, dau.
of J. Hopkins. Sur. George W. Hopkins. Wit. Henry Hopkins. Married 4 Mar. by Rev. Charles Hopkins. p 77

22 January 1779. John FULCHER and Mary Clark, dau. of
Elizabeth Clark. Sur. John Williams. Wit. Thomas Baley
and John Toney. p 22

27 December 1814. John FULCHER and Elizabeth Davis, dau.
of John Davis. Sur. Shelton G. Davis. Married 28 Dec.
by Rev. Lewis Chaudoin. p 122

5 May 1778. Richard FULCHER and Elizabeth Younger, dau.
of Ann Younger. Sur. John Fulcher. Wit. Daniel Grubb
and Jesse Clarkson. p 21

18 January 1794. William FUQUA and Jane Anderson, dau. of
Richard Anderson. Sur. William Sampson. Wit. Tarleton
Bates, Jed^h. Johnson, G. Johnson and Katy Anderson. Married 18 Jan. by Rev. Charles Hopkins. (Order Book 19,
p 582). Goochland County Marriage Register p 53

13 April 1803. William FUQUA and Polley Hooker, of age.
Sur. Francis L. Campbell. Wit. James Barnett. Married 14
April by Rev. Lewis Chaudoin. p 84

30 June 1778. Robert FURLONG and Mary Lee, dau. of John
Lee who is surety. Robert is of Cumberland County. p 21

22 September 1794. Edward FUZMORE and Rhoda Martin, of
age, dau. of Judith Fox. Sur. Thomas T. Bates. Wit.
Tarlton Bates and Charles F. Bates. Returned 15 December
by Rev. Lewis Chaudoin. p 54

23 December 1794. John GAFFING and Blendena Bowen. Married by Rev. Lewis Chaudoin. Goochland County Ministers'
Returns p 337

17 February 1779. Humphrey GAINES and Martha Bowles. Sur.
William Sharp Smith. Humphrey Gaines is of Albemarle
County. p 22

5 November 1799. Benjamin GAMMON and Sally Maddox, dau.
of Mary Maddox. Sur. William Maddox. p 72

14 February 1798. William GAMMON and Molly Johnson.
Sur. John Gammon. Married 15 Feb. by Rev. Lewis Chaudoin.
p 66

8 February 1810. Absalom GARTRIGHT and Nancy Pledge, dau.
of Ann Pledge. Sur. John W. Pledge. Wit. Arch. Pledge.
Married 8 Mar. by Rev. Samuel Woodfin. p 107

5 May 1800. James GATEWOOD and Anne George. William
George gives consent for Anne and he is surety. p 75

2 September 1802. John GATHRIGHT and Martha Redford,
(Patsey). Sur. John Laprade. p 81

18 December 1797. William GATHRIGHT and Jane Woodson, of
age. Sur. John Laprade. Wit. Jesse Read. William is under age. John Miller, of Henrico County, is his guardian.
Married 21 Dec. by Rev. William Webber. p 65

25 November 1767. James GEORGE, Jr. and Mary Swift, dau.
of William Swift. Sur. James Adams, of Albemarle County.
Wit. James George, Sr., Sarah Swift and Margarret Swift.
p 12

15 January 1772. Leonard GEORGE and Jenny Poor, dau. of
Thomas Poor. Sur. James George and George Payne, Jr.
Wit. Lucy Poor. p 16

16 April 1803. Robert GEORGE and Judith Hardin, dau. of
Thomas Hardin. Sur. James D. Shelton. Wit. John L. Harris and Elizabeth Hardin. Robert is son of James George.
p 84

12 June 1804. Robert GEORGE and Susanna Lacy, dau. of
Matthew Lacy. Sur. David M. Parrish. p 88

27 February 1813. William GEORGE, Jr. and Alice B. Payne,
dau. of Tarlton Payne. Sur. James Hopkins. Married 3
March by Rev. Lewis Chaudoin. p 118

14 September 1774. Thomas GIBSON and Martha Riddle, dau.
of Thomas Riddle who is surety. Wit. Charles May.
Samuel Ayers makes affadavit that Thomas, of Prince
Edward County, is of age. p 17

21 August 1809. John C. GILLIAM and Nancy P. Cocke, dau.
of James Cocke. Sur. David P. Cocke. p 104

23 December 1791. David GLASS and Betsey Massie, dau. of
William Massie. Sur. George Payne. Wit. Martin Copeland
and John Barnett. p 47

26 December 1806. James GLASS and Nancy Massie. Sur.
David Glass. Married 30 Dec. by Rev. Lewis Chaudoin.p 96

20 April 1795. John GLASS and Betsy Thurston. Sur. David Glass. Married 24 April by Rev. Lewis Chaudoin. p 56

15 June 1799. John GLASS and Clarissa Layne. Sur. James Glass. Married 20 June by Rev. Lewis Chaudoin. p 71

25 May 1790. Thomas GLASS and Mary Allen, of age, dau. of James Allen. Sur. Charles Massie. p 42

19 April 1791. Benjamin GLENN and Anne Thomas, dau. of Elizabeth Jennitt. Sur. William Hughes. Wit. John Hughes and Charles Terrell. p 45

24 October 1792. Robert GLENN and Salley Bowles. Married by Rev. Reuben Ford. (Order Book 19, p 327). Goochland County Marriage Register p 397

27 June 1774. James GORDAN and Anne Payne, dau. of Col. John Payne. Sur. Henry Armistead, of Lancaster County. James Gordon is of Lancaster County. p 17

28 June 1808. James GORDON and Eliza R. Redd. Sur. George Perkins. Wit. Mary Redd and Sally Redd. p 101

17 August 1783. John GORDON and Mary Rowntree, dau. of Randal Rowntree. Sur. John Curle. p 28

14 December 1812. William Henry GOWENS and Judith Attkisson. Sur. Pleasant Attkisson, Jr. p 116

19 October 1812. John GRANT and Mary Slayden. "Each of age and no objection on either side". Sur. Daniel Slayden. Wit. George W. Watkins and Preston Smith. Married 22 Oct. by Rev. Lewis Chaudoin who says John Grant, Jr. and Mary Sladyen. p 115

2 December 1802. Peter GRANT and Frances Ascue. Sur. John Farmer. Married 2 Dec. by Rev. Richard Pope. p 82

26 March 1807. James M. GRAVES and Polly M. Clements, dau. of Jesse Clements. Sur. Jesse Wilkinson. Married 14 April by Rev. Lewis Chaudoin. p 97

3 July 1743. Edmund GRAY and Mary Mayo. Sur. Joseph Dabbs. p 2

28 February 1787. James GRAY and Elizabeth Powell, dau. of William Powell. Sur. William Crouch. Married 3 March. (Deed Book 15, p 15). Goochland County Marriage Register p 36

8 March 1806. John GRAY and Catharine Chisholm, dau.of Walter Chisholm, Sr. Sur. Richard Cocke. Wit. Suprey Chisholm and Hen. Chisholm. p 93

4 November 1799. William GRAY and Jenney Guerrant, (also written Janey Guerrant), dau. of John Guerrant. Sur. Thomas Royster. Married 9 Nov. by Rev. William Webber who says Jane Guerrant. p 72

20 January 1808. John GREEN, Jr. and Peggy Thurston, dau. of Elizabeth Thurston. Sur. Noel Lowry. Wit. Donald Fraser. Married 27 Jan. by Rev. Lewis Chaudoin. p 99

28 September 1785. Joseph GREEN and Liddia Wood. Sur. Stephen Crouch. Married 30 Sept. (Deed Book 15, p 408). Goochland County Marriage Register p 31

21 July 1806. Thomas GREEN and Jane Attkison, dau. of Judith Attkison. Sur. Spotswood Childress. Wit. Nelson Childress. Jane's name is also written Jane Attkins on the bond. p 94

30 March 1813. Thomas GREEN and Polly Cheatham, dau. of John Cheatum. Sur. Robert Grooms. p 118

19 April 1813. John GREGORY and Keturah Clarke. Sur. Pleasant Clarke. Married 20 Apr. by Rev. Lewis Chaudoin. p 119

1 September 1798. William GRINSTEAD and Dorothea Lacy. Sur. Elliot Lacy. p 67

17 December 1792. John GROOM and Betsy Sanders. Sur. William Sanders. Married 18 Dec. (Order Book 19, p 434). Goochland County Marriage Register p 50

28 May 1810. Robert GROOM and Betsy Parrish. Sur. Micajah Parrish. Married 29 May by Rev. Lewis Chaudoin. p 107

24 May 1799. Edward GRUBB and Elizabeth Furlong. John Furlong, Sr. makes affadavit that Elizabeth "is the age of 21 years" and states that she resides with him, a relative. Sur. William Holman. Married 24 May by Rev. Richard Pope who says Edward Grubbs. p 71

12 January 1802. John GRUBBS and Christian Williams, of age. Sur. William Turner. p 80

13 February 1809. John GRUBBS and Jane Grant. Sur. John Grant. Married 15 Feb. by Rev. Lewis Chaudoin. p 103

15 April 1793. Daniel GUARRANT and Betsey Laprade, dau. of Susanna Laprade. Sur. Heath J. Miller. Wit. Susanna Tate. Married 20 April by Rev. Reuben Ford. (Order Book 19, p 582 says Daniel Guerrant). Goochland County Marriage Register p 51

17 July 1793. John N. HADEN and Susanna W. Payne, dau. of Agatha Payne. Sur. Jesse Haden. Wit. Sally Payne. Married 24 July. (Order Book 19, p 386). Goochland County Marriage Register p 52

27 January 1763. Zachariah HADEN and Elizabeth Poor. dau. of Thomas Poor. Sur. Obadiah Daniel. Wit. Milley Poor and Ann Poor. Joseph Haden, brother of Zachariah, makes affadavit that Zachariah "is 21 years of age or upwards". p 10

19 February 1760. John HALES and Elizabeth Miller. Sur. James Binford. p 8

19 December 1803. James HALL and Elizabeth Scott. Robert Taylor is Elizabeth's guardian. Sur. Anthony Layne or Stapleton Crutchfield. Wit. William Carter and William Taylor. Married 24 Dec. by Rev. Charles Hopkins. p 86

23 June 1799. John HALL and Milly Thomas, 21 years of age. Sur. Lewis Bourn. p 71

2 September 1765. Thomas HALL and Frances Williams, dau. of William Williams. Sur. John Todd, of Cumberland County. Wit. Sam Sherwin and John Gooch. Thomas is son of William Hall and is of Amelia County. p 11

13 October 1795. William W. HALL and Betsy Daniel, dau. of John and Sally Daniel. Sur. Ichabod Daniel. p 57

6 December 1794. Edward HALLAM and Mary Dabney,(Louisa). Married by Rev. Charles Hopkins. The bond for this marriage is in Louisa, dated 3 December 1794 and the Minister's return in Goochland County Ministers' Returns p 337

22 December 1795. Benjamin HALSALL and Elizabeth Lewis. Sur. John Lewis. p 58

16 March 1801. Benjamin HALSALL and Elizabeth Shelton. Sur. John Shelton. Married 7 Apr. by Rev. Charles Hopkins. p 78

14 February 1810. James HALSEY and Nancey Richards, dau. of William Richards. Sur. Francis Underwood. Married 15 Feb. by Rev. Lewis Chaudoin. p 106

11 April 1811. John HALSEY and Lucy Tiller. Married by Rev. Lewis Chaudoin. Goochland County Ministers' Returns p 317

18 October 1793. William A. HALSEY and Polly Lacy. Sur. Jesse Haden. Married 19 Oct. (Order Book 19, p 674 says William Allen Halsey). Goochland County Marriage Register p 52

4 December 1801. William HAMBY and Judith Johnson. Sur. Robert Jarratt. Married 5 Dec. by Rev. Lewis Chaudoin. p 79

22 May 1790. William HAMNER and Elizabeth Bradley. Sur. Walter Clopton. Married 23 May. (Deed Book 15, p 386). Goochland County Marriage Register p 42

14 April 1794. Major HANCOCK and Mary Page, dau. of William Page. Sur. William Miller. Wit. John Vaughan. Married 14 Apr. by Rev. Lewis Chaudoin. p 54

14 July 1806. Dabney HANES and Betsy Reddy, dau. of William Reddy. Sur. William Stone. Wit. Preston Smith. Married 17 July by Rev. Reuben Ford who says Elizabeth Reddy. p 94

24 May 1798. George HARDING and Elizabeth E. Baker, (Betsey). Samuel Aston makes affadavit that Elizabeth was born in 1775. Sur. Josiah Hatcher, Jr. Wit. Samuel Aston. p 66

12 May 1810. William HARDING and Polly Farrar, dau. of Frances Farrar. Sur. William Farrar, Jr. Wit. R. D. Hines. p 107

28 April 1800. George HARLOW and Caty Page, dau. of Mary Page. Sur. Booker Carrell. Married 1 May by Rev. Lewis Chaudoin. p 75

20 October 1806. George HARLOW and Polly Mullis, dau. of Anne Mullis. Sur. Lewis Page. Wit. Jo. Woodson. Married 23 Oct. by Rev. Lewis Chaudoin. p 95

2 July 1802. John HARRIS and Susannah Brown. John Brown makes affadavit that Susannah is an orphan and is of lawful age. Sur. James Garnett. p 81

16 February 1796. John L. HARRIS and Ann Shelton. Sur. John Shelton. Married 19 Feb. by Rev. John D. Blair who says Nancy Shelton. p 60

17 March 1782. Nathaniel HARRIS and Mary Howard. Sur. William Hicks. p 26

18 December 1785. Ralph HARRIS and Mary McCaul, dau. of Stokes McCaul. Sur. William McCaul. Wit. Redford Whitlow, Suanah Lacy, Thomas Williams, George Dabney and Claborne Duval. Ralph is son of William Harris. p 32

7 July 1812. Richard W. HARRIS and Nancy Lewis. Sur. John Dowdy. Wit. Alexander Kersey. p 115

16 October 1809. Samuel HARRIS and Lucy Smith, dau. of
Thomas Smith. Sur. George S. Smith. Wit. Sally Boyer.
Married 19 Oct. by Rev. Lewis Chaudoin who says Smyth.
p 105

18 October 1811. William HARRIS and Polly Chrismas.
Sur. James Ryan. Wit. George W. Watkins and M. Smith.
p 111

20 December 1797. Wingfield HARRIS and Sally Attkisson,
dau. of Sally Attkisson who is guardian of Wingfield.
Sur. Thomas Shelton. Wit. Richard Johnson and George
Hunter. Married 21 Dec. by Rev. Richard Johnson. p 65

7 November 1760. Carter Henry HARRISON and Susanna
Randolph, dau. of Isham Randolph, deceased. Sur. William Meriwether. Wit. Nicholas Meriwether. p 8

15 March 1790. Randolph HARRISON and Mary Randolph, dau.
of Thomas Randolph. Sur. Arch^d Randolph. Wit. John L.
Harris. p 42

16 February 1768. Thomas HARRISON and Mary Kannon, dau.
of Elizabeth Kannon and William Kannon, deceased. Sur.
William Harrison. p 12

26 December 1763. William HARRISON and Anna Payne, dau.
of Josias Payne. Sur. Robert Payne, Jr. Wit. William
Payne. p 11

10 November 1813. Samuel L. HART and Ann T. Curd, dau.
of John Curd. Sur. Thomas Curd. Married 10 Nov. by
Rev. Joseph D. Logan. p 120

21 March 1796. Thomas HASKINS and Elizabeth Smith.
Turner Clarke, Jr. makes affadavit as to her age and he
is surety. Married 21 Mar. by Rev. William Webber. p 60

18 August 1777. Gideon HATCHER and Martha Laprade, dau.
of John Laprade. Sur. Hezekiah Henley. Wit. Henry
Gray, Sr. and Henry Gray, Jr. p 19

21 November 1796. Josiah HATCHER, Jr. and Polly Johnson. D. Guerrant is Polly's guardian. Sur. William
Gray. Wit. J. L. Hatcher. Josiah, under age, is son
of Gideon Hatcher. Married 1 Dec. by Rev. William
Webber. p 61

27 January 1807. Josiah HATCHER and Nancy Sampson, dau.
of Richard Sampson. Sur. John Pollock. Married 29 Jan.
by Rev. Charles Hopkins. p 96

38

4 July 1788. William HATCHER and Jane L. Mayo. Sur.
Robert Mayo. p 40

8 June 1803. Thomas HATHHORN and Nancy Johnson. Sur.
Benjamin Johnson. Thomas is son of William Hathorn. p 84

17 May 1779. Daniel HAWES and Margaret Miller, "upwards of
21 years of age". Sur. Thomas Miller. Daniel, "upwards
of 21 years", is of Hanover County. Matthew Vaughan makes
affadavit as to the age of each party. p 22

8 December 1803. Elijah HAWKINS and Nancy Mitchell. Sur.
Meredith Cosby. p 85

10 May 1809. Jesse HAWKINS and Sally Sharp, Dau. of
Martin Sharp. Sur. William Poindexter. Wit. William
Ryan. Married by Rev. W. Cooke. Returned 11 Nov., 1809.
p 104

16 February 1798. Enoch HEAD and Charlotte Hume. Sur.
Alexander Hume. Married 16 Feb. by Rev. Richard Pope.
p 66

21 June 1771. William HEALE and Susanna Payne, dau. of
Josias Payne, the elder. Sur. George Payne, Jr. Wit.
Bourn Price, John Payne and Arch. Payne. George Robinson and George H. Opie make affadavit that William, "of
full age", is son of George Heale of Lancaster County.
p 15

8 November 1789. William HELMS and Betsy Slayden.
(Deed Book 15, p 318). Goochland County Marriage
Register p 395

20 February 1792. William HENDERSON and Peggy M. Hol-
man, dau. of James Holman. Sur. William Holman. Wit.
Charles Kerr. Married 1 Mar. (Deed Book 16, p 147 says
Peggyan Holman). Goochland County Marriage Register p 47

4 December 1811. Samuel O. HENDREN and Ann M. French, 21
years of age. Sur. Robert French. p 112

20 December 1800. Hezekiah HENLEY and Betsy Ford. Sur.
John Ford. p 76

10 March 1795. Leonard HENLEY and Milley Jordan, granddaughter of Hezekiah Puryear, her guardian. Sur. Thomas
Caldwell. p 56

17 January 1801. Patrick HENLEY and Polley Puryear, dau.
of Ann Puryear. Sur. Andrew Nuckols. Wit. William Puryear. (Is this a double wedding? See Andrew Nuckols).
p 77

4 December 1800. Turner R. HENLEY and Polly Cocke, dau. of Benjamin Cocke. Sur. Pleasant Cocke. p 76

26 November 1814. Turner R. HENLEY and Huldah Higgason, born 26 Sept. 1791, sister of Elizabeth Nowling. Sur. Daniel Wade, Jr. Wit. Richard McCard. p 122

1 October 1811. George HERNDON and Hannah Britt, dau. of William Britt. Sur. Thomas James. Wit. Martha Britt. Married 3 Oct. by Rev. Lewis Chaudoin. p 111

19 October 1812. James HERNDON and Ann Perkins, dau. of Arch^d. Perkins. Sur. Pleasant Turner. Married 30 Oct. by Rev. Lewis Chaudoin who says Ann R. Perkins. p 116

21 December 1773. John HERNDON and Mary Clarkson. Sur. Benjamin Herndon. Lewis Herndon makes affadavit that John is 21 years of age. p 17

15 December 1798. Thomas HERNDON and Susanna Britt. Sur. John Britt. Married 16 Dec. by Rev. Lewis Chaudoin. p 68

21 December 1795. John HICKS and Catey Herndon, dau. of John Herndon. Sur. Daniel Dismukes. Wit. William Holman and Walter Leake. p 58

16 June 1787. Meshack HICKS and Elizabeth Moreland. Sur. Wright Moreland. Meshack's name is also written Meshack Hix on the bond. Married 17 June by Rev. Reubin Ford. (Deed Book 15, p 14). Goochland County Marriage Register p 37

4 July 1786. Moses HICKS and Elizabeth Johnson. Sur. Meshack Hicks. p 34

11 May 1778. William HICKS and Elizabeth Harris, dau. of Harrison Harris. Sur. John Fulcher. Wit. Moses Hicks and William Adams. Mary Hicks gives consent for William. p 21

26 March 1803. David HIGGASON and Nancy Crenshaw, dau. of Morning Fretwell. Sur. Richard Fretwell. Wit. John Fretwell and John Jackson. David is son of Samuel Higgason. p 83

31 July 1804. Thomas HILL and Sarah Eldridge, dau. of Thomas Eldridge. Sur. John B. Eldridge. Wit. David Thomson. p 88

21 March 1785. Henry HINES and Nancy Bullock. Sur. Tarlton Hines. p 31

7 March 1788. James HINES and Elizabeth Graves. Sur.
Charles Fargerson. Married 10 April by Rev. William
Webber. (Order Book 19, p 328). Goochland County Marriage Register p 39

16 April 1804. Tarlton HINES and Polly Baugh, dau. of
Burwell Baugh. Sur. Daniel McLaren. p 87

19 September 1814. Abner HIX and Jane Matthews. Sur.
Edward Matthews. Married 22 Sept. by Rev. Lewis Chaudoin.
p 122

29 May 1807. John HIX and Kitty Cheatum, dau. of John
Cheatum. Sur. John W. Payne. Wit. William Turner.
Married 11 July by Rev. Lewis Chaudoin . p 97

16 December 1799. David HODGES and Nancy James. Sur.
William James. Married 21 Dec. by Rev. Lewis Chaudoin.
p 73

17 June 1808. James HODGES and Patsey Page, Sur. John
Page. Wit. James Page. Married 18 June by Rev. Lewis
Chaudoin. p 100

21 January 1788. Jesse HODGES and Susanna Page, dau. of
William Page. Sur. Johnson Hodges. p 39

25 December 1807. Jesse HODGES and Mary Thomas. Sur.
Richard Thomas. Wit. Charles Attkisson. Married 25 Dec.
by Rev. John James. p 99

16 September 1790. John HODGES and Frances Shelton, of
lawful age, dau. of Peter Shelton. Sur. George Payne.
Wit. Tarlton Bates. Married 17 Sept. (Deed Book 15,
p 487). Goochland County Marriage Register p 42

15 April 1785. Johnson HODGES and Elizabeth Mulles.
Sur. George Payne. Wit. Fleming Payne. p 31

11 December 1797. Joseph HODGES and Agnes Mims. Sur.
Robert Mims. Wit. Elizabeth Mims and Jane Mims. Married 12 Dec. by Rev. Lewis Chaudoin. p 64

2 July 1803. Thomas HODGES, Jr. and Nancy Ryan, dau. of
William Ryan. Sur. Richard Bates. Married 2 July by Rev.
Lewis Chaudoin. p 84

8 December 1795. William HODGES, Jr. and Elizabeth Cocke,
dau. of James Cocke. Sur. John Rutherford. Wit. Pleasant
Meredith and Mary Cocke. William is son of William Hodges,
Sr. of Louisa County. Married 9 Dec. by Rev. Charles Hopkins. p 58

4 September 1806. William HODGES, Jr. and Elizabeth Poor.
Sur. John James. Wit. Lewis Chaudoin. Married 4 Sept. by
Rev. Lewis Chaudoin. p 94

28 December 1814. William HODGES and Mary Daniel. Sur.
Thomas James. Married 29 Dec. by Rev. Lewis Chaudoin.
p 123

18 March 1786. Randolph HOLBROOK and Hannah Meanly. Sur.
Dennett Meanly. p 33

17 November 1786. Jesse HOLEBROOK and Susanna Meanly.
Elizabeth Meanly gives consent for Susanna. Sur. Peter
Walker. Wit. Richard Menely, Thomas Meriwether and
Francis Meanly. p 35

20 October 1769. James HOLEMAN and Sarah Miller, dau. of
William Miller. Sur. Anthony Martin, of Cumberland
County. Wit. William Miller, Jr. James, 21 years of age,
is son of John Holeman. p 14

27 August 1746. George HOLLAND and Sarah Ford. Sur.
Michael Holland. Wit. Valentine Wood. p 4

6 November 1779. George HOLLAND, jun^r. and Susannah
George, dau. of James George who is surety. Wit. Thomas
Nicholls and James Holland. George is son of George
Holland, Sr. p 23

21 December 1802. Hudson HOLLAND and Elizabeth F. Payne,
dau. of Tarleton Payne. Sur. Richard Bates. Wit. Fleming Payne and Johnne Payne. Married 21 Dec. by Rev.
Richard Pope. p 82

25 December 1810. Michael HOLLAND, Jr. and Patsey Clarke,
dau. of Mary Clarke. Sur. Henry Isbell. Michael is son
of Michael Holland, Sr. Married 27 Dec. by Rev. Lewis
Chaudoin. p 109

17 July 1786. Nathaniel HOLLAND and Susaa Clopton. Sur.
George Payne. Wit. Thomas Royster. p 34

17 May 1810. Nathaniel HOLLAND and Matilda Holland. Sur.
William Miller. Married by Rev. Leonard Page. p 107

30 December 1795. Thomas S. Holland and Sally Holland.
John Holland gives consent for Sally. Sur. George Goodloe. Wit. James Allen, Jr. p 59

7 April 1808. James HOLLOWAY and Sarah Ellis, dau. of
Stephen Ellis. Sur. Joseph S. Ellis. p 100

3 December 1800. George HOLMAN and Sally Holman, dau. of
Susannah Holman. Sur. John Britt. Married 4 Dec. by Rev.
Charles Hopkins. p 76

24 December 1807. William M. HOLMAN and Mary Heth Puryear.
Sur. Preston Smith. Married 24 Dec. by Rev. Lewis
Chaudoin. p 99

1 August 1783. James HOOD and Keziah Poor. Sur. Robert
Poor. p 28

12 November 1811. James HOOKER and Martha Jarrett, 21
years of age. Sur. Henry Cox. p 112

4 August 1812. Bartlett HOOMES and Elizabeth Cockran,
dau. of Henry Cockran. Sur. Jacob Martin. Wit. George
W. Watkins. Married 6 Aug. by Rev. Lewis Chaudoin.
p 115

1 April 1797. Joseph HOOPER and Elizabeth Sadler,(Betsy),
dau. of William Sadler. Sur. William Saunders. Wit. Nancey
Sadler. Married 1 April by Rev. Lewis Chaudoin. p 63

20 March 1797. Ephraim P. HOOTON and Mary Cardin. Sur.
Sherrard Parrish. Married 29 Mar. by Rev. Lewis Chaudoin
who says Mary Carder. p 62

27 February 1815. Moody J. HOPE and Elizabeth Parrish.
Sur. William Walker. p 123

28 November 1815. Thomas A. HOPE and Lucy B. Anderson,
dau. of Matthew Anderson. Sur. John B. Jones. Married
6 Dec. by Rev. Reuben Ford. p 126

11 December 1810. Anderson HOPKINS and Judith J. Johnson,
dau. of William Johnson. Sur. Collin Johnson. Wit.
George W. Watkins. Married 11 Dec. by Rev. Lewis
Chaudoin. p 108

30 March 1798. Benjamin HOPKINS and Nancy Toler. Sur.
Richard Toler. Married 31 Mar. by Rev. Charles Hopkins.
p 66

13 July 1811. Capt. Charles HOPKINS and Ann Woodson,
dau. of Sally Woodson. Sur. William Johnson. Wit. Polly
Woodson. Married 13 July by Rev. lewis Chaudoin. p 110

21 December 1810. Garland HOPKINS and Sophia Lovell, dau.
of Elizabeth Lovell. Sur. George Phillips. Married 22
Dec. by Rev. Lewis Chaudoin. p 109

43

21 May 1801. George W. HOPKINS and Elizabeth French,
dau. of Saley French. Sur. Mason French. Wit. Robert
French. p 78

15 June 1815. Joseph HOPKINS and America A. Talley. Sur.
John Pollock. Married 17 June by Rev. J. D. Logan. p 125

7 December 1802. Nelson HOPKINS and Polly Matthews, dau.
of Sharod Matthews. Sur. Anderson B. Matthews. Wit.
Richard Bates. Married 30 Dec. by Rev. Charles Hopkins.
p 82

14 December 1792. William HOPKINS and Anne Cocke. Sur.
Benjamin Cocke. Married 15 Dec. (Deed Book 16, p 130).
Goochland County Marriage Register p 50

3 November 1806. William HOPKINS and Salley M. Massie.
Sur. Gideon Massie. p 95

15 July 1815. Patterson HOPPER and Catharine Glass, "21
years of age in April last". Sur. Robert Mims. Wit.
Lucy D. Jarrett and Martha A. Mims. Married 16 July by
Rev. Lewis Chaudoin. p 125

1 January 1785. James HOUCHENS and Mary Scrugs. Sur.
Richard Scrugs. p 31

28 June 1782. Francis HOUCHIN and Mary Jones. Married
by Rev. Reuben Ford. Goochland County Ministers' Returns p 392

1 May 1807. Charles HOUCHINS and Sarah Bruce. Sur.
John Bradshaw, Jr. Married 2 June by Rev. Lewis
Chaudoin. p 97

23 October 1785. Edward HOUCHINS and Nancy Clements.
Sur. Jesse Clements. p 275

4 January 1810. Edward HOUCHINS and Judith Osborne.
Sur. Richard Thomas. Married 4 Jan. by Rev. Lewis
Chaudoin. p 106

1 January 1802. Jesse HOUCHINS and Susanna Pace. Sur.
James Clements. Wit. Joseph Pace. Married 2 Jan. by
Rev. Richard Pope. p 80

14 November 1792. John HOUCHINS and Delphia Muse, dau.
of William Muse. Sur. James Clements. Married 15 Nov.
(Deed Book 16, p 175). Goochland County Marriage Register p 49

8 February 1799. Joshua HOUCHINS and Deborah Mims.
Sur. James Clements, Jr. Married 9 Feb. by Rev. Lewis
Chaudoin. p 70

16 October 1797. George HUBARD and Patsy Cardin. John
Perkins gives consent for Patsy. Sur. Robert Carden.
Wit. Richard Bates. Married 19 Oct. by Rev. Lewis
Chaudoin. p 64

27 August 1806. Daniel HUBBARD and Frances Attkisson,
dau. of Josiah Attkisson. Sur. Thomas Attkison. Married
28 Aug. by Rev. Charles Hopkins. p 94

24 December 1812. Daniel HUBBARD and Judy Madison Powers.
Sur. John W. Powers. p 117

9 December 1802. George HUBBARD and Mary Merin. Sur.
John Foster. Wit. John Davis. Married 9 Dec. by Rev.
Lewis Chaudoin. p 82

12 September 1801. Garrard Morgan HUDDLESTON and Nancy
Page. Sur. Reuben Page. Wit. Richard Bates. Garrard's
name is also written Jarrot Morgan Huddleston on the bond.
Married 17 Sept. by Rev. Lewis Chaudoin. p 79

16 June 1788. David HUDSON and Mary Clopton. Sur. Benjamin Clopton. p 39

9 July 1792. George HUDSON and Nancy Holland, dau. of
John Holland. Sur. Tarlton Payne. Married 13 July.
(Deed Book 16, p 175). Goochland County Marriage Regis-
ter p 48

5 August 1788. Benjamin HUGHES and Mary Johnson. (Deed
Book 15, p 240). Goochland County Marriage Register p
394

17 November 1800. Benjamin HUGHES and Lucy Farrar. Sur.
John Ford. p 76

14 June 1784. William HUGHES and Sarah Harding. Sur.
Thomas Harding. Wit. Thomas Puryear. p 29

13 June 1815. William HUGHES and Jane W. Sanders, dau.
of William Sanders. Sur. Nelson A. Sanders. Wit. Turner A. Saunders. Married 15 June by Rev. Reuben Ford
who says Jane W. Saunders. p 124

20 September 1789. Benjamin HUGHSON and Jane Johnson.
(Deed Book 15, p 318). Goochland County Marriage Register p 394

25 February 1796. John HUGHSON and Hannah Johnson.
Sur. Benjamin Johnson. Married 25 Feb. by Rev. William
Webber. p 60

13 March 1794. David HUMPHREYS and Susanna Thurston.
Sur. William Thurston. Wit. W. Miller. Married 13 Mar.
(Order Book 19, p 674). Goochland County Marriage Register p 54

6 February 1809. Allen HUNTER and Rhoda Anderson, dau.
of Meridith Anderson. Sur. John Lawrence. Married 9
Feb. by Rev. Lewis Chaudoin. p 103

6 March 1815. Austin ISAACS and Susan Pierce. Sur.
Samuel Martin. Married 6 Mar. by Rev. Lewis Chaudoin.
p 124

4 November 1787. Henry ISAACS and Mary Banks. Sur.
Josiah Leake. p 38

13 December 1803. Christopher ISBELL and Elizabeth Woodson. Sur. John Woodson. Wit. Austin Walker and Joseph
Woodson. Married 15 Dec. by Rev. Charles Hopkins. p 85

30 October 1792. Thomas D. ISBELL and Ann Poindexter
Kerr. Sur. Charles Kerr. Married 1 Nov. (Deed Book
16, p 130). Goochland County Marriage Register p 49

11 July 1791. Ed. M. JACKSON and ___ ___. Sur.
Cuffy Payne. Married 12 July. (Deed Book 16, p 38
says Edmund M. Jackson and Polly Martin). Goochland
County Marriage Register p 45

9 December 1806. Elisha JACKSON and Sarah Swift, dau.
of Clevears Swift, deceased. William Mills was executor of her father's estate. Sur. Thomas Bowles. Wit.
Charles Swift and W. K. Bowles. p 95

29 May 1800. Frederick JAMES and Dorothea Anne Dandridge, dau. of W. Dandridge. Sur. William S. Dandridge. Wit. Arch^d. B. Dandridge. p 75

6 November 1800. James JAMES, Jr. and Judith Howell,
dau. of Aise (Isaac) Howell. Sur. Junior Howell. Married 7 Nov. by Rev. Lewis Chaudoin. p 76

19 January 1807. John JAMES and Polly Poor. Sur. William Hodges, Jr. Wit. Preston Smith. Married 26 March
by Rev. Lewis Chaudoin. p 96

9 December 1813. Richard JAMES and Mary G. Poor, dau.
of Thomas Poor. Sur. Martin James. Wit. James Poor.
Married 18 Dec. by Rev. Lewis Chaudoin. p 120

18 December 1780. David JARRATT and Anna Wade, dau. of
William Wade, deceased. Sur. Deveraux Jarratt. p 25

25 January 1793. Devereaux JARRATT and Christian Humber.
Sur. John Humber, Jr. p 51

20 November 1788. Thomas JARROTT and Susanna Thompson.
Charles and Elizabeth Johnson give consent for Susanna.
Sur. Robert Jarratt. Thomas Jarrott is also spelled
Thomas Jarratt on the bond. p 40

3 October 1739. Peter JEFFERSON and Jane Randolph. Sur.
Arthur Hopkins. Wit. H. Wood. p 1

26 October 1815. Anthony JENKINS and Jane Dobbins. Sur.
Austin Isaacs. Married 27 Oct. by Rev. Lewis Chaudoin.
p 125

27 December 1815. Lewis JENKINS and Sally Jenkins. Sur.
Anthony Jenkins. Married 28 Dec. by Rev. Lewis Chaudoin.
p 127

27 December 1808. James JENKS and Elizabeth Morrisett.
Daniel Wade is Elizabeth's guardian. Sur. Ambrose Wade.
p 103

11 June 1791. Edward JENNINGS and Martha Hines. (Deed
Book 16, p 37). Goochland County Marriage Register p 396

9 November 1793. John JENNINGS and Caty Lowry, 27 years
of age. Sur. William Colvard. Married 10 Nov. by Rev.
Reuben Ford. (Order Book 19, p 582 says Keturah Loury).
Goochland County Marriage Register p 52

31 March 1813. William JETT and Anna Bates, dau. of
Caroline W. Bates. Sur. John Spears. Married 1 April
by Rev. Joseph D. Logan. p 118

8 October 1805. Benjamin JOHNS and Elizabeth Salmon,
dau. of John Salmon who is surety. Wit. Samuel Branch.
Married 10 Oct. by Rev. Lewis Chaudoin who says Elizabeth Salmons. p 91

5 October 1809. James JOHNS and Susanna Lemay. Sur.
Samuel Lemay. Married 12 Oct. by Rev. Lewis Chaudoin.
p 105

1 September 1779. Benjamin JOHNSON and Anna Norvell,
dau. of James Norvell. Sur. John Johnson. Wit. William
Haden. Benjamin is son of Joseph Johnson. p 23

28 December 1784. Benjamin JOHNSON and Rachael Pace.
Sur. Francis Pace. p 30

17 February 1783. Charles JOHNSON, Jr. and Mary Ann
Farrar. Sur. Stephen Crouch. p 27

15 June 1814. Charles J. JOHNSON and Susan H. Hughson, dau. of John Hughson. Sur. John Harris, Jr. p 121

14 January 1788. Clabourn JOHNSON and Anna Johnson. Sur. David Johnson, Jr. p 39

7 October 1793. Curtis JOHNSON and Sarah Brag. Sur. Murray Pace. Wit. Edward Pace. p 52

31 January 1778. Daniel JOHNSON and Anne Baughn. Sur. Elisha Leak. p 20

10 August 1794. Daniel JOHNSON and Jenny Riddle, dau. of Thomas Riddle. Sur. Reuben Turner. Wit. Joseph W. Riddle. Married 28 Aug. by Rev. Charles Hopkins. p 54

16 December 1790. David JOHNSON and Nancey Bowles. (Deed Book 15, p 487). Goochland County Marriage Register p 396

25 August 1807. Elijah JOHNSON and Martha Carter, 21 years of age, dau. of Mary Carter. Sur. Pleasant Cocke. Wit. Thomas Carter. p 98

18 April 1798. Isham JOHNSON and Nancy Ricks, dau. of Nicholas Ricks. Sur. Forris Hunter. Wit. Gilbert Ricks. Married 20 Apr. by Rev. Richard Pope. p 66

9 December 1791. John JOHNSON and Jane Eldridge, dau. of Thomas Eldridge. Sur. Daniel Johnson. Married 10 Dec. by Rev. Reuben Ford. (Order Book 19, pp 327 & 582). Goochland County Marriage Register p 47

29 March 1804. John JOHNSON and Molly Johnson. Sur. Benjamin Johnson. p 87

22 December 1808. John JOHNSON and Mary Pace, dau. of Robert Pace. Sur. Lemuel Toler. Married by Rev. Leonard Page. Returned 18 February 1810. p 103

15 May 1809. John JOHNSON and Patsy Watkins, dau. of Joseph D. Watkins. Sur. Milner Woodson. p 104

17 May 1787. Joseph JOHNSON and Betsy Anderson, dau. of Benjamin Anderson. Sur. Martin Mims. Wit. Robert Mims, Stephen Clements and Mary Clements. p 36

17 October 1792. Knuckles JOHNSON and Susanna Perkins. The bond for this marriage is found in Louisa County and the above record is found in Goochland Deed Book 16, p 175. Goochland County Marriage Register p 397

24 October 1787. Manoah JOHNSON and Mary Mantlo. John Mantlo makes affadavit that Mary was born 30 Jan. 1760. Sur. Elisha Leake. p 38

18 April 1785. Richard JOHNSON and Milly Walker. Sur. Shadrack Walker. p 31

14 March 1799. Richard JOHNSON and Elizabeth Lacy, dau. of Elliot Lacy who is surety. p 70

26 August 1806. Richard JOHNSON and Polly Denton, dau. of John and Suzanar Denton. Sur. Spotswood Childress. Wit. John Denton, Jr. p 94

12 November 1803. Robert JOHNSON and Elizabeth G. Dabney. Sur. James D. Shelton. Wit. John L. Harris. p 85

13 October 1789. Stephen JOHNSON and Anna Rountree. Married 13 Oct. by Rev. William Webber. (Order Book 18, p 328). Goochland County Marriage Register p 400

14 September 1795. Stephen JOHNSON and Polly W. Pope, dau. of Thomas Pope. Sur. John S. Johnson. p 57

16 October 1801. Stephen JOHNSON and Sarah Burch, dau. of Margaret Burch. Sur. Philip Lawson. p 79

18 May 1782. Thomas JOHNSON and Catherine Madocks. Sur. Jesse Lacy. p 26

22 March 1787. Thomas JOHNSON and Judith Peers. Sur. Benjamin Johnson, Jr. Married 7 April by Rev. Reuben Ford. (Deed Book 15, p 14). Goochland County Marriage Register p 36

13 October 1802. Thomas JOHNSON and Nancy Lawrence. Sur. John Rutherford. Married 13 Oct. by Rev. Richard Pope. p 82

5 January 1804. Thomas JOHNSON and Nancy Johnson, dau. of Charles Johnson. Sur. John Hughson. p 86

15 October 1781. William JOHNSON and Nancy Johnson. Sur. Benjamin Johnson. p 25

14 December 1784. William JOHNSON and Elizabeth Woodson, dau. of Mary Woodson. Sur. Pearin Redford. Wit. Benjamin Woodson. p 30

18 August 1788. William JOHNSON and Susanna Holland. Sur. Edward Matthews. p 40

20 July 1792. William JOHNSON and Polley Webber. Married 2o July by Rev. Reuben Ford. (Order Book 19, pp 327 & 582). See William Johnson. Goochland County Marriage Register p 397

11 September 1792. William JOHNSON and Polly Webber. William Webber gives consent for Polly. Sur. Mitchel Martin. Wit. John Bryers. (See William Johnson). p 48

12 December 1792. William JOHNSON and Mary Britt, dau. of John Britt. Sur. James Maddox. Wit. Martin Key. Married 13 Dec. (Deed Book 16, p 175). Goochland County Marriage Register p 49

7 August 1795. William JOHNSON and Mary Watkins, dau. of Benjamin Watkins, deceased. She is "of lawful age". Sur. Daniel Johnson. Married 24 Sept. by Rev. Charles Hopkins. p 57

19 September 1796. William JOHNSON and Judith Jarratt. Sur. Robert Jarratt. Married 4 Oct. by Rev. Hugh French. p 61

29 December 1798. William JOHNSON and Salley Toler, dau. of George Toler. Sur. Forris Hunter. Wit. George Profitt and George Hudson. Married 29 Dec. by Rev. Richard Pope. p 69

10 August 1810. William JOHNSON and Martha S. Poor. Sur. John R. Boatwright. Wit. Thomas Poor. Married 16 Aug. by Rev. Lewis Chaudoin. p 107

2 November 1812. William JOHNSON and Jane E. Clarke, dau. of Turner Clarke, Jr. Sur. James Hopkins. Wit. Bolling Britt. Married 3 Nov. by Rev. Lewis Chaudoin. p 116

24 November 1795. William L. JOHNSON and Phebe Cocke. Sur. Christopher Stanley. Wit. John C. Payne. Married 25 Nov. by Rev. Charles Hopkins. p 58

16 June 1788. Peter JOHNSTON and Mary Wood. Sur. Stephen Southall. Wit. Sher^d. Parrish. p 39

30 January 1805. Dabney H. JONES and Salley Layne, dau. of John Layne. Sur. George Layne. Married 31 Jan. by Rev. Lewis Chaudoin. p 89

1 August 1799. David JONES and Nancy Brown. Sur. Thomas Shomaker. Married 3 Aug. by Rev. William Webber. p 72

14 December 1790. Drewry JONES and Polly Barnett, dau. of William Barnett. Sur. John Barnett. Wit. Robert Barnett. Drewry Jones is of Henrico County. p 44

29 November 1791. Frederick JONES and Lucy Leake. Sur. Walter Leake. Married 30 Nov. (Deed Book 16, p 37). Goochland County Marriage Register p 46

10 August 1807. Samuel JONES and Patsey Seldon Chick,
dau. of William Chick. Sur. William H. Jones. Samuel
is son of David Jones, Sr. of Hanover County. p 98

30 January 1798. James JORDAN and Elizabeth Wade, dau.
of Robert Wade. Sur. Archer Evans. Wit. John Jordan and
Stephen Crouch. p 66

18 November 1799. John JORDAN and Sarah Martin, dau. of
John Martin. Sur. John Thurman. Wit. Sherod Lain and
John Gilbert. p 72

25 October 1813. Matthew JORDAN and Martha Brown. Sur.
Daniel Brown. p 120

-- February 1744. Samuel JORDAN and Judith Ware. Sur.
Thomas Ballard Smith. p 3

16 November 1771. William JORDAN and Elizabeth Woodson,
dau. of Joseph Woodson. Sur. Matthew Jordan. Wit. James
Jordan, Samuel Jordan, Joseph Woodson, Jr. and John Hines.
William is son of Charles Jordan, Sr. p 16

20 April 1812. Obediah JORDON and Jane Morrison. Sur.
John Morrison. Wit. George W. Watkins. p 114

21 August 1784. John JOUETT, Jun[r]. and Sarah Robards.
Sur. Lewis Robards. Wit. Nicholas Lewis. p 29

18 January 1801. Reubin JOURDEN and Phebe Wingfield.
Sur. Leonard Balleu. Reuben's name is also written
Reubin Jordan on the bond. p 77

15 September 1800. Andrew KEAN and Kitty Vaughan. Sur.
 William Miller. Married 17 Sept. by Rev. Charles Hopkins. p 75

24 March 1800. Samuel KEININGHAM and Sarah Perkins, dau.
of Arch[s] Perkins who makes affadavit that Sarah is "of
lawful age". Sur. Grief Perkins. Married 26 Mar. by Rev.
Charles Hopkins. p 75

15 November 1783. John KELSHER and Sarah Parrish, dau.
of Aaron Parrish. Sur. Fleming Payne. p 28

8 December 1811. James KELSO and Elizabeth Halsall,
Sur. Pleasant Cocke. p 112

11 January 1763. James KENNADAY and Sarah Hodges, dau.
of Welcome William Hodges. Sur. John Norvell and Jesse
Hodges. James Kennaday, also written James Cannaday, is
of Augusta County. George Stevenson makes affadavit that
James is "21 years of age or upwards". p 10

9 November 1812. John KENNON and Sarah Morris. Sur.
Robert Morris. Married 6 Dec. by Rev. Lewis Chaudoin.
p 116

3 April 1744. William KENNON, Jr. and Elizabeth Lewis,
dau. of Charles Lewis. Sur. John Lewis, Jr. Wit. Robert
Morgan. p 3

17 November 1810. Henry KERSEY and Salley Tate. Sur.
William Poindexter. Wit. Alex[n] Kersey. Married 20 Nov.
by Rev. W. Cooke. p 108

9 October 1776. John KEY and Nancy Ford, "age 17 years",
dau. of Thomas Ford. Sur. Joshua Key, of Albemarle
County. Wit. Sarah Roundtree and Nancy Childres. John
Key is of Albemarle County. p 18

18 December 1797. Martin KEY and Betsy Johnson. Sur.
Charles Johnson. Married 21 Dec. by Rev. Lewis
Chaudoin. p 65

10 February 1812. Robert KEY and Jane C. Clements, dau.
of Jesse Clements. Sur. Wilson Cardin. Wit. James
Graves. Married 12 Feb. by Rev. Lewis Chaudoin. p 114

27 December 1815. Higgason KING and Polly Waldrop, 21
years of age. Sur. Francis Waldrop. p 127

18 December 1815. Peter KING and Nancy Foster. David
Richardson, who is surety, makes affadavit that Nancy is
over 21 years of age since her guardian has ceased to
act for her. Higgason King is guardian of Peter King,
"of age". p 126

16 September 1797. Ambrose KNIGHT and Arpasia Vaughan.
Mary Vaughan gives consent for Arpasia. Sur. James
Vaughan, Jr. Married 10 October by Rev. Reuben Ford.
p 64

17 August 1795. Stephen LACY and Polley B. Holland. Sur.
George Holland. Wit. W. Miller. Married 27 Aug. by Rev.
Richard Pope. p 57

13 August 1802. Jesse LAINE and Frances Wingfield. Sur.
Joshua Woodward. Jesse's name is also written Jesse Lane
on the bond. p 81

16 April 1810. John H. LANG, Jr. and Polly C. Lawrence.
Sur. George W. Parrish. See John H. Long. p 107

17 June 1760. John LAPRADE and Susanna Wadlow, dau. of
Thomas Wadlow. Sur. William Miller. Wit. Joseph Starkey
and Elizabeth Starkey. p 8

6 July 1771. John LAWRENCE and Mary Ann Powers, dau. of James Powers, deceased. Sur. Jolly Parrish. John, who was 21 years of age the 6th of Sept. 1770, is son of Elizabeth Lawrence. p 15

19 December 1808. John LAWRENCE, Jr. and Polly Terry. Sur. Fr. Underwood. Wit. Lawrence Anderson. Married 20 Dec. by Rev. Lewis Chaudoin. p 102

2 May 1787. William LAWRENCE and Charity Parrish. Aaron and Sary Parrish give consent for Charity. Sur. John Lawrence. William is "of lawful age". p 36

12 June 1787. Anthony LAYNE and Anne Craddock. Sur. John Bevans. p 37

22 February 1808. Claibourne LAYNE and Sally Glass. Sur. James Glass. Married 25 Feb. by Rev. Lewis Chaudoin. p 100

9 February 1778. David LAYNE, Junr and Katcread Farish. Sur. David Layne. p 20

31 August 1807. Elisha LAYNE and Elizabeth W. Layne, dau. of Tarlton Layne. Sur. Thomas James. Wit. Martin James. Married 31 Aug. by Rev. John James. See Elisha Layne. p 98

3 September 1807. Elisha LAYNE and Elizabeth W. Layne. Married by Rev. John James. (There are TWO entries with same names on the same page in Ministers' Returns). See Elisha Layne. Goochland County Ministers' Returns p 315

20 October 1792. Frederick LAYNE and Judith Barker. Sur. Robert Poor. Married 2 November. (Deed Book 16, p 147). Goochland County Marriage Register p 49

20 August 1804. George LAYNE and Salley Gilliam, dau. of John Gilliam. Sur. Washington Drumwright. Wit. Elizabeth Parrish. Married 28 Aug. by Rev. Lewis Chaudoin. p 88

2 February 1797. Henry M. LAYNE and Nancy Clarke. Sur. Stephen Nowlin, Jr. p 62

21 November 1796. Jacob B. LAYNE and Nancy Bradshaw. Sur. Learner Bradshaw. Married 17 Dec. by Rev. Richard Pope. p 61

4 March 1786. John LAYNE and Mary Crafton. David Crenshaw, of Hanover County, is Mary's guardian. Sur. Drury Williams. p 33

31 July 1811. Thomas LAYNE and Catharine Utley, dau. of
Hezekiah Utley. Sur. Obediah Utley. p 110

13 July 1786. William LAYNE and Frances Dowdy, dau. of
Elizabeth Dowdy. Sur. Richard Johnson. p 34

22 June 1786. William LAYNE and Elizabeth Dowdy. (Deed
Book 15, p 14). Goochland County Marriage Register p 393

22 November 1809. Woodson LAYNE and Susanna Holland,
dau. of George Holland. Sur. George Layne. Married 23
Nov. by Rev. Lewis Chaudoin. p 105

23 March 1791. Elisha LEAKE and Fanny Curd. Sur. Thomas
Hatcher. Married 26 March. (Deed Book 15, p 487).
Goochland County Marriage Register p 44

22 March 1799. Josiah LEAKE and Elizabeth P. Hatcher.
Sur. John Quarles. Married 23 Mar. by Rev. Charles Hopkins. p 70

30 September 1790. Walter LEAKE and Susanna Jones. Sur.
James Quigg. Married 1 October. (Deed Book 15, p 487).
Goochland County Marriage Register p 43

19 December 1796. Edward LEE and Polly James, dau. of
William James who is surety. Married 22 Dec. by Rev.
Lewis Chaudoin. p 62

3 July 1788. John LEE and Jane Tuggle. Sur. Henry Tuggle. Wit. Richard Payne. Married 5 July. (Deed Book
15, p 240). Goochland County Marriage Register p 39

11 October 1808. John S. LEE and Elizabeth Puryear.
Sur. John Smith. p 101

5 December 1788. Kendall LEE and Judith B. Payne. Sur.
William Miller. Wit. Joseph Myers. p 40

31 March 1795. Stephen LEE and Betsey Strong. Sur.
Nathan Strong. Married 2 April by Rev. Lewis Chaudoin.
p 56

26 September 1780. William LEE and Jane Payne, dau. of
John Payne, the elder. Sur. John K. Read. Wit. James
Gordon. William Lee is of Northumberland County. p 24

15 January 1810. David LEMAY and Polly Martin. Sur.
Francis Underwood. Wit. David Massie. Married by Rev.
Lewis Chaudoin. p 106

13 August 1785. Samuel LEMAY and Agnes Massie. Sur.
William Walker. p 31

3 December 1802. Samuel LEMAY and Agnes Bailey, dau. of
Callom Bailey. Sur. Thomas Hodges. p 83

22 December 1791. Peter LESUEUR and Sarah Williams.
(Deed Book 16, p 37). Goochland County Marriage Register
p 397

20 January 1767. Stephen Giles LETCHER and Elizabeth Perkins. Sur. Joseph Perkins. p 12

15 July 1746. Charles LEWIS, Junr. and Mary Randolph.
Sur. Valentine Wood. p 3

28 April 1780. Howel LEWIS and Betsey Coleman, dau. of
Robert Coleman, who is surety. Wit. James Terry and
James Johnson. Howel, 21 years of age the 2nd of April
1780, is son of Howell Lewis, Sr. This is in a letter
written from Granville County, North Carolina. p 24

16 April 1784. Howell LEWIS and Ann Bolling, dau. of
John Bolling. Sur. Robert Lewis, Jr. Wit. John Bolling, Jr. and John Woodson, Jr. p 29

6 November 1790. John LEWIS and Sally Utley, dau. of
William Utley. Sur. Stephen Crouch. Wit. Richard Lewis
and Phil Webber. Married 6 Nov. by Rev. William Webber.
(Order Book 19, p 328). Goochland County Marriage Register p 43

11 December 1793. John LEWIS, Jr. and Jane Cocke. Sur.
Thomas Cocke. Wit. Benjamin Cocke. Married 12 Dec. by
Rev. Charles Hopkins. (Order Book 19, p 582). Gooch-
land County Marriage Register p 52

2 September 1797. Lilburn LEWIS and Betsey Lewis, dau.
of Robert Lewis. Sur. William Price. Married 6 Sept. by
Rev. William Calhoon. p 64

17 January 1791. Randolph LEWIS and Mary H. Lewis.
Sur. George Holman. p 44

16 December 1792. Richard LEWIS and Mary Potter. Sur.
Turner Clarke, Jr. Wit. Jacob Johnson. Married by Rev.
William Webber. (Order Book 19, p 328). Goochland
County Marriage Register p 50

19 February 1760. Robert LEWIS and Jane Woodson. Sur.
Thomas Bolling. p 8

25 April 1809. Robert LEWIS and Ann Ragland, dau. of
Dudley Ragland. Sur. James Hopkins. Warner Lewis is
guardian of Robert, his nephew. Married 26 Apr. by Rev.
Lewis Chaudoin. p 104

31 August 1760. Robert LEWIS, Jr. and Frances Lewis, dau. of Col. Charles Lewis. Sur. Robert Lewis. Wit. David Meriwether, Pichey Ridgway Gilmer, Francis Meriwether and John Lewis. Robert is son of Robert Lewis who is brother of Col. Charles Lewis. p 8

10 May 1786. Robert LEWIS, Jr. and Mary G. Bryce, dau. of Archibald Bryce. Sur. Andrew Ware. Robert is son of Col. Robert Lewis. p 33

19 September 1801. Stephen LEWIS and Judith Gordon. Sur. Stephen Crouch. Wit. William Lewis and Benjamin Gordin. p 79

1 June 1758. Thomas LEWIS and Susanna Ellis, dau. of John Ellis. Sur. Joseph Ellis. Wit. Valentine Wood. p 7

5 June 1798. Warner LEWIS and Sally P. Woodson, dau. of Samuel Woodson. Sur. Robert H. Woodson. Married 7 June by Rev. Charles Hopkins. p 67

8 February 1774. William LEWIS and Sally Mann, of age, dau. of Mary Mann. Sur. John Philpotts. William Pryor makes affadavit that William Lewis is 21 years of age. p 17

15 November 1799. William LEWIS and Fanny Gordon, dau. of John Gordon. Sur. Stephen Crouch. Wit. William Gordin and Benjamin Gordin. p 72

8 July 1807. Richard LIGON and Susanna C. Bernard. Sur. John Bernard. Married 15 July by Rev. Lewis Chaudoin. p 97

18 February 1791. John LILE and Fanny Scott, dau. of Elizabeth Scott. Sur. Elisha Sym. Married 26 Feb, (Deed Book 16, p 34). Goochland County Marriage Register p 44

16 February 1801. John LOCKNANE and Nancy Gordon, dau. of John Gordon. Sur. Philip Woodson. p 77

17 December 1814. Lawrence LODGE and Sarah Underwood, dau. of Elizabeth Underwood. Sur. William Lewis. Married 17 Dec. by Rev. Lewis Chaudoin. p 122

15 December 1794. James LOGAN and Mary Strong. Ann Strong gives consent for Mary. Sur. Josiah Carrell. Married 15 Dec. by Rev. Lewis Chaudoin. p 55

3 October 1812. Rev. Joseph D. LOGAN and Jane Dandridge. Sur. George Woodson Payne. Married 8 Oct. by Rev. Conrad Speece. p 115

19 April 1810. John H. LONG and Polly C. Lawrence. Married by Rev. Lewis Chaudoin. See John H. Lang, Jr. Goochland County Ministers' Returns p 317

28 January 1807. Joseph H. LONG and Nancy Hodges, dau. of Frances Hodges. Sur. Henry Attkins. Wit. Robert Hodges. p 96

17 July 1797. William LOVELL and Betsy Shepard. James Shapard gives consent for Betsy. Sur. William Lovell. p 63

19 December 1808. Abraham LOVING and Rachel Strong, dau. of Nathan Strong. Sur. Thomas Strong. Wit. Nathan Strong, Jr. Married 24 Dec. by Rev. Lewis Chaudoin. p 103

28 December 1792. Gabriel LOVING and Salley Norvell, dau. of Thomas Norvell. Sur. Joseph Faris. Wit. William Miller. Married 29 Dec. (Deed Book 16, p 147). Goochland County Marriage Register p 50

14 December 1809. James LOWRY and Sally Crutchfield. Sur. Isaac Murry. Married 27 Dec. by Rev. Lewis Chaudoin. p 105

28 December 1811. William LOWRY and Polly Crutchfield, of age. Sur. William Bush. Married 26 February 1812 by Rev. Lewis Chaudoin who spells the name, Loury. p 113

27 September 1794. Thomas LOYDE and Elizabeth Hodges. Sur. Thomas Hodges. Married 28 Sept. by Rev. Charles Hopkins. p 55

24 December 1799. Francis LUDDINGTON and Ursula Woodson. Sur. Charles F. Bates. Married 25 Dec. by Rev. Hugh French. p 73

29 July 1801. Thomas LYNCH and Sally Banks, born 2nd July 1779, dau. of John Banks. Sur. Edward Fuzmore. Married 29 July by Rev. Richard Pope. p 78

21 August 1815. Thomas LYNCH and Frances Faudree, dau. of Thomas Faudree. Sur. John G. Childress. p 125

13 February 1807. James McALISTER and Jo Anne Gray, dau. of Susanna Gray. Sur. Charles Hopkins, Jr. Married 14 Feb. by Rev. Charles Hopkins who says James McAllister. p 97

15 October 1787. Daniel Mac ALLISTER and Susannah Woodward, dau. of Susannah Woodward. Sur. William Attkisson. Wit. Thomas Shoemaker and Samuel Woodward. Daniel's name is also written Daniel Macallister. p 37

5 August 1815. Howell McBRIDE and Polly Drumwright, dau. of Capt. George Drumwright. Both are of age. Sur. Major Sladgen. Wit. John Underwood. Married 5 Aug. by Rev. Lewis Chaudoin. p 125

10 September 1802. John McBRIDE and Charlotte Graves. John Harvie makes affadavit that Charlotte is an orphan and has lived in his home since early youth. Sur. Rufus Soule. Wit. John Harvie, Jr. p 81

1 January 1807. John McBRIDE and Harriott Lee. Married by Rev. Charles Hopkins. Goochland County Ministers' Returns p 350

25 November 1797. Minor McBRIDE and Milly Adams. Sur. Nathaniel Burford. Married 25 Nov. by Rev. Charles Hopkins. p 64

25 September 1780. Richard McBRIDE and Frances Moss, dau. of John Moss, Jr. who is surety. p 24

11 January 1803. Robert McBRIDE and Polly Blunakall. Sur. William **Blunkall**. p 83

25 December 1792. Daniel McCARY and Patsey Johnson. Sur. Thomas Martin. Married 25 Dec. (Deed Book 16, p 175). Goochland County Marriage Register p 50

7 May 1787. Richard McCARY and Nancy Martin. Sur. William Martin. p 36

22 March 1809. Stoakes McCAUL and Ann Webb. Sur. William Miller. p 104

22 October 1798. Neal McCOOK and Nancy Rowen. Sur. Joseph Attkisson. Married 25 Oct. by Rev. Charles Hopkins. p 68

27 May 1806. Neil McCOULL and Julia Logan. James Carter is Julia's guardian. Sur. William Miller. Wit. M. Hunnicutt and Harriot Logan. Married 1 June by Rev. Charles Hopkins. p 93

9 October 1787. Daniel McCOY and Jane Parrish. Sur. William Burgess. p 37

4 December 1792. John McCRAY and Nancy Lowry, dau. of Mathew Lowry, Sr. Sur. Mathew Lowry, Jr. Wit. William Mullins. p 49

5 June 1815. Benjamin McDONALD and Nancey George "alias Cooper". Jo Woodson makes affadavit that Nancy is of age and an orphan. Sur. James Cockran. Benjamin McDonald is a "free man of color". Married 8 June by Rev. Lewis Chaudoin. p 124

8 October 1814. John McKEAND and Mary Gilliam. Sur.
Thomas Branch. Married 8 Oct. by Rev. Lewis Chaudoin.
p 122

21 October 1791. Robin McNUCKOLDS and Susanna Martin.
Sur. Ned Martin. Married 21 Oct. (Deed Book 16, p 34
says Robin Metuckolds and Susanna Martin). Goochland
County Marriage Register p 46

17 December 1789. John MADDOCKS and Ellinor Aston. Married 17 Dec. by Rev. William Webber. (Order Book 19,
p 328). Goochland County Marriage Register p 395

7 October 1789. Jacob MADDOX and Mary Maddox. (Deed
Book 15, p 478). Goochland County Marriage Register
p 394

15 February 1808. James MADDOX and Mary Johnson. Sur.
William Johnson. p 100

17 October 1796. Jesse MADDOX and Christian Johnson,
21 years of age. Sur. Stephen Johnson. Wit. Benjamin
Johnson and Thomas Pope. Married 27 Oct. by Rev. Hugh
French. p 61

18 December 1802. William MADDOX and Jane Johnson. Edward Matthews is Jane's guardian. Sur. John Tinsley.
Wit. David Mastin, James Tiller and James Sammons. p 82

24 December 1789. Wilson MADDOX and Betsey Smith. (Deed
Book 15, p 478). Goochland County Marriage Register p 395

15 August 1814. Fleming MALLORY and Judith Mallory, dau.
of Sally Mallory. Sur. Thomas Dickerson. Married 31
Aug. by Rev. Lewis Chaudoin. p 122

11 December 1807. Overton MALLORY and Peggy Austin, dau.
of John Austin. Sur. Fleming Austin. Wit. Peter
Attikisson. p 98

17 December 1787. Stephen MALLORY and Mary Bowles, dau.
of Gideon Bowles. Sur. Gwathmey Dabney. Wit. Sarah
Bowles. p 38

28 November 1795. Joseph MANGUM and Elizabeth Humber,
dau. of John Humber, Sr. Sur. Edward Cox, Jr. Married
29 Nov. by Rev. Charles Hopkins. p 58

23 April 1795. Moses MANN and Sarah Lewis. Sur. John
Lewis. Married 25 Apr. by Rev. Charles Hopkins. p 57

6 February 1813. Moses MANN and Elizabeth Ann Attkisson, dau. of Charles Attkisson. Sur. Benjamin B. Duke. p 118

16 February 1795. James MANTELOW and Lucy Wade. Sur. Daniel Wade. Married 16 Feb. by Rev. William Webber. p 56

13 July 1791. Edward MARTIN and Polly Martin, dau. of Suke Martin. Sur. ----- None given. Edward gives his own consent. p 280

9 March 1779. John MARTIN and Lucy Layne, dau. of Jacob Layne. Sur. Abram Parrish. Wit. Thomas Martin and Charles Goodmon. p 22

17 March 1813. John MARTIN and Rebecca Argyle. Married by Rev. Joseph D. Logan. See John Mastin. Goochland County Ministers' Returns p 354

2⁰October 1786. Mitchel MARTIN and Jeny Clarke. Sur. William Martin. Married 20 Oct. by Rev. Reuben Ford who says Jenny Clearke. (Deed Book 15, p 14). Goochland County Marriage Register p 35

5 May 1804. Nathan MARTIN and Elizabeth Bradshaw. Sur. John Bradshaw. Married 12 May by Rev. Lewis Chaudoin. p 87

15 November 1815. Nelson MARTIN and Eliza Jones. Sur. George Southworth. p 126

24 December 1798. Robert MARTIN and Judith Moore, dau. of Amos Lᵈ. Moore. Sur. Reubin Pleasants. Wit. John Moore and J. Witt. p 69

15 December 1803. Samuel MARTIN and Elizabeth Witt. Sur. Benjamin Witt. p 86

7 March 1808. Samuel MARTIN and Nancy Isaacs. Sur. Francis Cousins. Married 10 Mar. by Rev. Lewis Chaudoin. p 100

24 February 1810. Thomas MARTIN and Polly Nowlin, dau.of Stephen and Ann Nowlin. Sur. Robert Martin. p 106

18 June 1787. William MARTIN and Anne Green. Sur. Sherwood Parrish. p 37

7 December 1805. William MARTIN and Mary Ann Page. Sur. Dabney Page. p 91

1 January 1811. William MARTIN and Judith Jenkins. Sur. James Shelton. William Martin is "a man of color". Married 2 Jan. by Rev. Lewis Chaudoin. p 109

16 February 1785. Charles MASSIE and ____ ____. Sur.
William Martin. Wit. Fleming Payne. p 31

8 March 1815. David MASSIE and Polly Michie, dau. of
John Michie. Sur. William Miller. p 124

14 May 1806. Gideon MASSIE and Susanna Smith Puryear.
Sur. Thomas Miller. Married 14 May by Rev. Charles
Hopkins. p 93

14 September 1747. Thomas MASSIE and Susanna Holland.
Sur. Henry Martin. p 4

25 June 1776. Thomas MASSIE and Elizabeth Massie, dau.
of Nathaniel Massie. Sur. William Massie. Wit. Frances
Massie. Nathaniel Massie is guardian of Thomas, who is
"of age". p 18

18 January 1797. Thomas MASSIE and Sally Parrish, dau.
of Humphrey Parrish. Sur. Dabney Parrish. Wit. George
Parrish and Fleming Payne. Married 19 Jan. by Rev.
Charles Hopkins. p 62

17 March 1813. John MASTIN and Rebecca Argyle. Sur.
Thomas W. Pollock. See John Martin. p 118

20 April 1772. Edward MATHEWS and Jane Watkins, Junr.,
dau. of Jane Watkins. Sur. Stephen Sampson. Wit. Joseph
Watkins, Thomas Watkins and Susanna Watkins. Edward
Mathews is also written Edward Matthies on the bond. p 16

3 April 1807. Thomas MATHEWS and Elizabeth Toler. Sur.
George Toler. Married 1 May by Rev. Lewis Chaudoin. p 97

12 April 1791. Benjamin MATTHEWS and Alcey Johnson,
(Ealsey Johnson), dau. of Benjamin Johnson. Sur. Edward
Matthews. Wit. T. Bates. Married 15 April. (Deed Book
15, p 488 says Alice Johnson). Goochland County Marriage
Register p 44

18 March 1795. Bradley MATTHEWS and Mary Redd. Married by
Rev. William Webber. Goochland County Ministers' Returns
p 339

24 May 1815. James MATTHEWS and Alsey Hix, dau. of Thomas Matthews, Jr. Wit. William Whitlock. Married 25
May by Rev. Lewis Chaudoin. p 124

26 September 1789. John MATTHEWS and Nancy Peers. (Deed
Book 15, p 478). Goochland County Marriage Register
p 394

1 December 1808. Thomas MATTHEWS and Charlotte Fulcher.
Joseph Hooper makes affadavit that Charlotte is 21 years
of age. Sur. William Pledge. Wit. John Fulcher. Married 12 Jan. 1809 by Rev. John James, Baptist Minister.
p 102

16 December 1811. William MATTHEWS, Jr. and Elizabeth
Brill. Sur. Edward Matthews. (See William Matthews,Jr.
p 113

26 December 1811. William MATTHEWS, Jr. and Elizabeth
Britt. Married by Rev. Lewis Chaudoin. (See William
Matthews, Jr.). Goochland County Ministers' Returns
p 318

18 March 1795. Bradley MATTHIS and Mary Redd. Sur. Paul
Dismukes. p 56

17 May 1813. William M. MAY and Mary S. Fowler, dau. of
Alexander Fowler. Sur. Jacob B. Fowler. Married 2 June
by Rev. Lewis Chaudoin. p 119

6 December 1815. Elias L. MAYO and Polly Isbell. Sur.
Stephen Mayo. Wit. George Drumwright. Married 7 Dec.
by Rev. Lewis Chaudoin. p 126

5 February 1812. James W. MAYO and Roxy Ann Layne.
"Fathers of both parties are present". (No names are
given). Sur. Anthony Layne. p 114

4 February 1783. Stephen MAYO and Ann Isbell. Sur.
Edward McBride. p 27

2 July 1799. Tom MAYO and Abbey Cousins. Sur. Joseph
Attkisson. p 71

3 January 1803. James MEALEY and Frankey Scott. Sur.
William Scott. Married 6 Jan. by Rev. Lewis Chaudoin.
p 83

22 May 1740. William MEGGINSON and Mary Goode. Sur.
Arthur Hopkins. Wit. Joseph Dabbs. p 1

27 July 1793. Pleasant MEREDITH and Mary Cocke, born
October 24, 1758. Sur. John Lewis. Wit. Nancy Cocke,
Jun. and Anne Cocke. Married 27 July by Rev. Reuben
Ford. (Order Book 19, p 582). Goochland County Mar-
riage Register p 52

29 October 1768. George MERIWETHER and Martha Meriwether. Sur. William Meriwether. p 13

6 September 1762. James MERIWETHER and Elizabeth Pol-
lard, dau. of Joseph Pollard. Sur. William Meriwether.
Wit. William Colvard. James Meriwether is of Louisa
County. p 10

27 December 1760. Nicholas MERIWETHER and Margaret Doug-
lass, dau. of Rev. William Douglass. Sur. Benjamin Mosby.
Wit. Nich^S. Douglass and Margareat Huddleston. Nicholas
Meriwether is of Louisa County. p 9

19 August 1805. Robert MERIWETHER and Martha Pryor, dau.
of William Pryor. Sur. Turner R. Whitlock. p 91

1 July 1751. William MERIWETHER and Patty Wood, dau. of
Henry Wood. Sur. Valentine Wood. Wit. Thomas Walker
and James Coleman. Nicholas Meriwether is guardian of
William. p 6

12 July 1795. Jesse MERRIAN and Elizabeth Henderson.
Sur. Anthony Lane. Jesse Merrian is a widower. Married
16 July by Rev. Lewis Chaudoin who says Betsy. p 57

6 May 1793. Jesse MERRIAN and Nancy Halbird, dau. of
Mary Keeps(?). Sur. Clarkson Maddox. Jesse's name is
also written Jesse Marin on the bond. p 51

26 November 1792. John MERRIN and Mary Hall, dau. of
Jeney Hall. Sur. Clarkson Maddox. p 49

17 March 1782. David MICHEL and Betsy Cosby. Sur.
George Payne. Wit. Robert Coleman. p 26

30 _____ 1749. William MICHELL and Agnes Payne, dau. of
Josias and Ann Payne. Sur. James Gresham. Wit. Thomas
Starke. p 5

21 November 1785. Heath J. MILLER and Elizabeth Guerrant. Sur. William H. Miller. p 32

3 April 1792. John MILLER and Sally Jordan, dau. of
James Geirden, deceased, and Sarah Geirden. Sur. William Williams. Wit. John Jorden and Phillip Tinsley.
Married 9 April by Rev. William Webber. (Order Book 19,
p 328). Goochland County Marriage Register p 47

18 February 1799. John MILLER and Margaret Richardson,
dau. of George Richardson. Sur. William Miller. Married 20 Feb. by Rev. Hugh French who says Peggy Richardson. p 70

29 September 1800. John C. MILLER and Polly H. Holman.
Sur. William Holman. Married 2 Oct. by Rev. Lewis
Chaudoin. p 76

28 December 1786. Thomas MILLER and Constance Massie.
Sur. Nathaniel Massie. p 35

7 June 1803. William MILLER and Ann Lewis Redford. Sur.
John Curd. Married 8 June by Rev. Charles Hopkins. p 84

16 March 1772. William MILLER, Jr. and Johanna Laprade,
dau of John Laprade. Sur. George Richardson. p 16

10 February 1808. Jackson MILLS and Martha O. Ragland,
dau. of Dudley Ragland. Sur. James Ragland. Wit.
Nathaniel Burruss. Married 15 Feb. by Rev. Lewis
Chaudoin. P 100

30 October 1804. Duiguid MIMS and Martha Massie. Sur.
Gideon Massie. Married 1 November by Rev. Charles Hopkins. p 88

5 April 1788. Robert MIMS and Lucy Poor. Sur. James
Poor. Wit. Abraham Poor. Married 6 April. (Deed Book
15, p 240). Goochland County Marriage Register p 39

5 September 1810. Robert MIMS and Rebeckah Massie. Sur.
John L. Harris. Wit. Martha Mims, D. Mims and Thomas
Hood. Married 6 Sept. by Rev. Lewis Chaudoin. p 108

27 March 1756. Benjamin MITCHEL and Ann Massie, widow
of David Massie, deceased. Sur. William Perkins. Wit.
William Mossley and Susannah Robards. p 7

10 December 1808. Cary MITCHELL and Sally Powers. Sur.
Major Powers. p 102

19 October 1812. John MITCHELL and Elizabeth Cardin,
dau. of Robert Cardin. Sur. William Davis. Married 22
Oct. by Rev. Lewis Chaudoin who says Elizabeth Carden.
p 116

21 December 1781. William MITCHELL and Jane Britt, dau.
of William Britt. Sur. George Payne. Wit. Harden Burnley, Jr. p 26

21 December 1807. William MITCHELL and Mary Magdaline
Le May, dau. of Samuel Le May. Sur. Francis Underwood.
Wit. Archelaus Mitchell and David Lemay. p 99

25 January 1799. John MOORE and Patsy Martin, dau. of
Samuel Martin. Sur. Robert Martin. Wit. J. Witt. p 70

23 January 1796. Summerset MOORE and Sarah Powers, dau.
of William Powers. Sur. Charles Attkisson. p 59

22 October 1790. Charles MORELAND and Susanna Hancock, dau. of Major Hancock. Sur. Joel Ryan. Married 23 Oct. (Deed Book 15, p 452). Goochland County Marriage Register p 43

30 September 1790. Thomas MORELAND and Sarah Thomas, dau. of James Thomas. Sur. Arch^d. Pleasants. Wit. Major Hancock. Married 2 October. (Deed Book 15, p 452). Goochland County Marriage Register p 43

29 April 1797. Thomas MORELAND and Elizabeth Page, 21 years of age, dau. of Mary Page and sister of James Page who is surety. Married 29 Apr. by Rev. Lewis Chaudoin. p 63

4 July 1782. Wright MORELAND and Sarah Hancock. Married by Rev. Reuben Ford. Goochland County Ministers' Returns p 392

24 May 1806. Edward MORRIS and Susanna Johns. Sur. Harris Nichols. Wit. Preston Smith. (See Edward Morris). p 93

10 July 1806. Edward MORRIS and Susanna Johnson. Married by Rev. John James. (See Edward Morris). Goochland County Ministers' Returns p 315

21 January 1799. George MORRIS and Mary Smith. Sur. John Smith. Married 22 Jan. by Rev. Hugh French. p 69

20 September 1779. John MORRIS and Sarah Preyear. Sur. Giles Harding who makes affadavit that John is of lawful age. p 23

5 December 1804. John MORRIS and Nancy Faris. Sur. Devereux Jarratt. Married 8 Dec. by Rev. Lewis Chaudoin. p 89

18 November 1799. Joseph Royall MORRIS and Mary Nicholson. Sur. Thomas Eldridge, Jr. Joseph is of Henry County. Married 23 Nov. by Rev. Charles Hopkins. p 73

4 August 1788. Capt. Nathaniel G. MORRIS and Mary Woodson, dau. of John Woodson. Joseph Woodson, her uncle, makes affadavit as to her age and, with Francis Pledge, is surety. Wit. John S. Woodson. p 21

17 August 1783. William MORRISETT and Ann Farrar. Sur. Robert Farrar. p 28

15 February 1796. William MORROW and Elizabeth P. McDonald. Sur. Angus McDonald. Married 17 Feb. by Rev. Charles Hopkins. p 59

10 April 1799. John MOSBY and Jenny Ware, dau. of John
Ware. Sur. James Ware. Wit. John Ware, Junr. and Mildred Ware. Married 11 Apr. by Rev. Charles Hopkins. p 70

19 October 1795. Langston MOSBY and Lucy Turner,(also
written Mrs. Lucy Turner on the bond). Sur. William
Turner. p 58

9 August 1748. Littleberry MOSBY and Mrs. Elizabeth
Netherland. Wade Netherland makes affadavit for Mrs.
Netherland. Sur. John Netherland. Wit. Mary Fleming.
Littleberry is son of Benjamin Mosby. Mrs. Netherland
gives her own consent. p 4

10 June 1747. Micajah MOSBY and Maudlin James. Sur.
Stephen Bedford. p 4

26 April 1749. Robert MOSBY and Ann Lewis, dau. of
Joseph Lewis. Sur. William Robards. (See Robert Mosby).
p 5

24 April 1769. Robert MOSBY and Ann Lewis, dau. of
Joseph Lewis. Sur. Joseph Lewis and John Lewis. (See
Robert Mosby). p 13

22 January 1806. James MOSELEY and Mourning T. Mallory.
Sur. Richard A. Dandridge. Wit. William Moseley and John
Hutsin. Married 23 Feb. by Rev. Reuben Ford. p 92

18 October 1787. William MOSELEY and Susannah Jordan.
Married by Rev. George Smith, Baptist . The bond for
this marriage is in Powhatan County and the above data
is in Goochland County Ministers' Returns p 313

26 December 1795. Marvel Adams MOSLEY and Nancy Jennings,
dau. of Samuel Jennings. Sur. Thomas T. Bates. Wit. William Lovell. p 58

18 December 1810. Benjamin MOSS and Hannah Baker. Sur.
Richard Moss. Married 22 Dec. by Rev. Lewis Chaudoin.
p 108

29 October 1812. Daniel MOSS and Lucy Pierce. Sur.
Joseph Gray. Married by Rev. Lewis Chaudoin. p 116

1 January 1762. Gideon MOSS and Susanna Richardson.
Sur. Robert Richardson. p 9

1 June 1768. Hugh MOSS and Fanny Ford, dau. of Thomas
Ford. Sur. William Ford. Wit. Absalom Howle. p 13

5 January 1801. James W. MOSS and Mary Woodson, dau.
of Josiah Woodson. Sur. Matthew Woodson. p 77

30 December 1780. Nathaniel MOSS and Johannah Johnson. Sur. Samuel Moss. Wit. Matthew Lacy and William Rutherford. p 25

10 November 1800. William MOSS and Betsy Cheattum. Sur. James Bibb. Wit. Richard Pope and Janey Pope. Married 10 Nov. by Rev. Richard Pope. p 76

30 August 1781. David MULLINS and Rosanna Herndon. Sur. James Williams. p 25

3 July 1788. Jesse MULLINS and Elizabeth Cocke. (Deed Book 15, p 240). Goochland County Marriage Register p 394

27 January 1804. William MULLINS and Elizabeth Toler, 21 years of age. Sur. Benjamin Bradshaw. Married 27 Jan. by Rev. Lewis Chaudoin. p 87

28 September 1763. Drury MURRELL and _____ Rountree. Sur. William Rountree. Drury Murrell is of Louisa County. p 11

26 December 1793. Stephen MURRELL and Elizabeth Haden, the younger. Capt. Sampson is Elizabeth's guardian. Sur. William Sampson. Married 27 Dec. by Rev. Charles Hopkins. (Order Book 19, p 582). Goochland County Marriage Register p 53

24 May 1797. John MURRER and Betsy Mitchell, of lawful age - 30 years -, dau. of Anne Mitchell. Sur. Benjamin Murrer. John's name is also written John Morrow on the bond. Married 26 May by Rev. Richard Pope. p 63

1 August 1795. Thomas MURRER and Elizabeth Farmer. Sur. Thomas Farmer. Married 1 Aug. by Rev. Lewis Chaudoin who says Betsy. (Is this a double wedding? See John Farmer). p 57

31 May 1784. Samuel MURRILL and Susanna Puryear. Sur. Hezekiah Puryear. p 29

18 July 1786. William MUSE and Susanna Johnson. Sur. John Martin. p 34

6 February 1812. James W. MYERS and Roxey Ann Layne. Married by Rev. Lewis Chaudoin. Goochland County Ministers' Returns p 353

17 October 1793. John NEAVES and Milly Winn Puryear. Married by Rev. William Webber. Goochland County Ministers' Returns p 339

23 August 1803. Samuel NELSON and Mrs. Elizabeth Crank, dau. of Jane Hall. Sur. William W. Hall. p 84

24 May 1806. Harris NICHOLS and Nancy Scott. Sur. Edward Morris. Married 29 May by Rev. John James who says Nancy is daughter of Joseph Scott. p 93

8 June 1814. Henry W. NICHOLS and Lucy M. Price. Sur. John Pollock. Wit. Mary A. Moody. Married 9 June by Rev. Lewis Chaudoin. p 121

18 December 1782. Matthew NIGHTINGALE and Judith Perkins. Sur. Madison Power. p 27

14 November 1807. Matthew NIGHTINGALE, Jr. and Sarah Hooker. Sur. William Lane. Wit. Jacob Woodson and Faney Bernard. p 98

23 September 1811. John B. NOOE and Mrs. Harriet T. Burnley, dau. of Daniel Triplett. Sur. William Miller. Wit. John R. Triplett. John B. Nooe is of Madison County. p 111

17 July 1809. Daniel NORRIS and Constantine P. Gilliam. Sur. George Layne. Married 25 July by Rev. Lewis Chaudoin who says Constance. p 104

1 February 1779. Thomas NORVELL and Judith Parrish, dau. of William Parrish. Sur. Gideon Bowles. p 22

16 February 1788. Abram NOWLIN and Mildred Watkins. Sur. Thomas Watkins. p 39

17 October 1784. David NOWLIN and Ann Powell, dau. of William Powell. Sur. Daniel Aston, (also written Daniel Ashton on the bond). p 30

19 December 1800. David NOWLIN and Susanna Crouch. Sur. Stephen Woodson. Married 20 Dec. by Rev. Charles Hopkins. p 76

17 June 1782. Stephen NOWLING and Susanna Clarke. Married by Rev. Reuben Ford. Goochland County Ministers' Returns p 392

6 November 1789. Stephen NOWLING and Ann Witt. (Deed Book 15, p 478). Goochland County Marriage Register p 394

17 January 1801. Andrew NUCKOLS and Patsy Puryear, dau. of Ann Puryear. Sur. Patrick Henley. Wit. William Puryear. (Is this a double wedding? See Patrick Henley). p 77

68

7 March 1801. Andrew Knight NUCKOLS and Martha Graves.
Sur. Rice Graves. Wit. James Graves. Married 8 Mar. by
Rev. Charles Hopkins. p 78

3 April 1813. Benjamin NUCKOLS and Elizabeth J. Toler,
dau. of Mary Toler. Sur. Spotswood Childress. p 119

12 January 1796. John NUCKOLS and Elizabeth Nuckols,
dau. of Pouncy Nuckols. Sur. Charles Nuckols. Wit.
Richard Childress. John is son of William Nuckols. p 59

24 December 1812. Jonathan NUCKOLS and Elizabeth Childress,
21 years of age, dau. of William Childress. Sur. William
A. Nuckols. p 117

8 December 1813. Nathan NUCKOLS and Polly M. Cary. Sur.
Nelson Nuckols. p 120

18 March 1811. Nelson NUCKOLS and Polly Reddy. Sur.
Overton Nuckols. p 110

3 February 1801. Obadiah NUCKOLS and Elizabeth Willis,
dau. of Sarah Willis. Sur. Spotswood Childress. Wit.
Mary Bartlett. p 77

8 January 1811. Overton NUCKOLS and Agnes Going. Sur.
Robert Blunkall. p 109

14 June 1815. Pouncy NUCKOLS, Jr. and Martha M.
Nuckols. Sur. Benjamin Cocke, Jr. Married 15 July by
Rev. Reuben Ford. p 124

7 November 1804. Thomas NUCKOLS and Nancy Nuckols.
Sur. Overton Nuckols. p 89

23 October 1797. William NUCKOLS and Nancy Barnett,
dau. of William Barnett. Sur. Charles Nuckols. Wit.
John Nuckols, John Barnett and Elisha Barnett. William is son of Pouncey Nuckols. Married 26 Oct. by
Rev. William Webber. p 64

21 January 1804. William NUCKOLS and Martha Nuckols,
dau. of Pouncey Nuckols. Sur. John Nuckols. p 87

25 August 1809. William NUCKOLS and Nancy W. Puryear,
21 years of age. Sur. Benjamin Nuckols. p 104

19 July 1792. Archelaus NUNREY and Elizabeth Hopper,
dau. of Tabitha Hopper. Sur. Bartlett Cox. Wit. Turner Clarke, Jr. Married 19 July. (Deed Book 16, p 130).
Goochland County Marriage Register p 48

29 August 1758. Richard OGLESBY and Elizabeth Curd,
widow of John Curd, deceased. Sur. Stephen Perkins. p 7

26 September 1789. Zachariah OLVIS and Elizabeth Webster.
(Deed Book 15, p 478). Goochland County Marriage Register p 394

18 August 1813. David A. OWEN and Polly Dinue, dau. of
Larrose Dimue. Sur. John Crenshaw. Married 21 October
by Rev. Lewis Chaudoin who says Polly Dimue. p 120

11 August 1805. Elisha OWEN and Ritta Gill. Sur. George
Bowles. p 91

21 June 1796. Robert OWEN and Kitty Leake, dau. of
Elisha Leake. Sur. Josiah Leake. Married 21 June by
Rev. Charles Hopkins. p 60

20 September 1784. Edward PACE and Susannah Johnson.
Sur. Jesse Pace. Wit. G. Payne and James Curd. p 273

17 August 1795. James PACE and Lydia Drake, dau. of
Sary Drayke. Sur. Wilson Maddox. Wit. Benjamin Johnson and Frances Pace. p 284

28 October 1813. James PACE and Susanna Mitchell, 21
years of age. Sur. Robert S. Smith. Married 28 Oct. by
Rev. Lewis Chaudoin. p 305

19 May 1806. Jesse PACE and Catharine Pace, (Cyty).
Joseph Pace gives consent for each party. Sur. William
W. Hall. Married 21 May by Rev. Lewis Chaudoin. p 296

19 January 1795. Joseph PACE and Elizabeth Clements,
dau. of John Clements. Sur. John Guerrant, Jr. Married 28 Jan. by Rev. Lewis Chaudoin. p 283

4 January 1790. Robert PACE and Frances Tuggle. Sur.
John Lee. Married 5 January (1790). (Deed Book 15,
pp 385 & 452). Goochland County Marriage Register p 279

1 May 1805. William PACE and Lucy Pace, dau. of Jesse
Pace. Married 4 May by Rev. Lewis Chaudoin. p 294

10 October 1789. Anderson PAGE and Fanny Williams.
(Deed Book 15, p 318). Goochland County Marriage Register p 394

4 December 1805. Benjamin PAGE and Martha Hodges, (Patsy),
dau. of William Hodges. Sur. Lewis Page. Married 5 Dec.
by Rev. Lewis Chaudoin. p 295

8 April 1801. Dabney PAGE and Elizabeth Hancock. Sur.
Major Hancock, Jr. Wit. Richard Bates. Married 8 Apr.
by Rev. Lewis Chaudoin. p 290

19 November 1800. James PAGE and Sarah Hancock, dau. of
Major Hancock. Sur. Major Hancock. Married 20 Nov. by
Rev. Lewis Chaudoin. p 289

27 December 1810. James PAGE and Jane Salmon. Sur.
James Salmon. Married 27 Dec. by Rev. Lewis Chaudoin
who says <u>Jane Salmons</u>. p 301

3 February 1806. Jesse PAGE and Polly Alvis, "upwards
of 21 years", dau. of George Alvis, deceased. Sur. William
Page. Married 6 Feb. by Rev. Lewis Chaudoin. p 296

30 October 1800. John PAGE and Anner Pace. Sur. William
Miller. Married 30 Oct. by Rev. Lewis Chaudoin. p 288

24 July 1804. John PAGE and Elizabeth Sims, widow. Sur.
James Adams. Wit. Benjamin Anderson. p 293

16 May 1809. John PAGE and Polly Salmons. Sur. John
Salmons. Married 18 May by Rev. Lewis Chaudoin. p 300

18 November 1805. Lewis PAGE and Nancy Hodges, dau. of
Johnson Hodges. Sur. Leonard Page. Wit. W. Miller. p
294

3 September 1803. Mann PAGE and Polly Hancock. Sur.
Major Hancock, Jr. Married 8 Sept. by Rev. Lewis
Chaudoin. p 292

12 March 1811. Pleasant PAGE and Janey Page, dau. of
Leonard Page. Sur. Jesse Page. Married by Rev. Leonard
Page. p 301

24 October 1789. Robert PAGE and Sally Harding. (Deed
Book 15, p 478). Goochland County Marriage Register
p 394

2 April 1791. William PAGE and Milley Hopper, dau. of
Milley Hopper. Sur. Jesse Hodges. Married 7 April.
(Deed Book 15, p 487). Goochland County Marriage
Register p 280

11 February 1793. William PAGE and Elizabeth Witt, dau.
of Mary Witt. Sur. William Miller. Wit. Jesse Witt.
p 282

15 December 1794. William PAGE and Nancy Page, dau. of
John Page. Sur. David Sanders "or David Saunders".
Wit. Stephen Lane. p 283

5 April 1798. William PAGE and Christian Hodges, dau.
of Lewcy Hodges. Sur. Jesse Hodges. Married 5 April
by Rev. Lewis Chaudoin. p 287

27 February 1806. William PAGE and Elizabeth Alvis, dau.
of George Alvis, deceased. Sur. James Johnson. Married
27 Feb. by Rev. John James. p 296

24 December 1781. Martin PALMER and Elizabeth Powers,
dau. of William Powers. Sur. Madison Powers. Wit. Wm.
Atkins. p 272

-- November 1785. Thomas PANKEY and Martha Cannon. Sur.
James Johnson. p 275

5 October 1790. Corbin PARISH and Elizabeth Parrish.
(Deed Book 15, p 432). Goochland County Marriage
Register p 395

15 December 1806. Allen PARRISH and Elizabeth A. Thomas.
Sur. William Parrish. Wit. Meredith Parrish. John Parrish gives consent for Allen Parrish. p 297

8 December 1813. Benjamin PARRISH and Polly H. Groomes
Sur. Peyton H. Bailey. Married 8 Dec. by Rev. Lewis
Chaudoin. p 305

19 September 1808. Booker Smith PARRISH and Martha T.
Gilliam, under age, dau. of John Gilliam. Sur. George
Layne. Married 22 Sept. by Rev. Lewis Chaudoin. p 299

17 July 1786. Cager PARRISH and Dolly Parrish. Sur.
Sherwood Parrish. p 276

18 June 1796. Carter PARRISH and Permilia Parrish, dau.
of Anne Parrish. Sur. Micajah Parrish. Wit. Corbin
Parrish and Fred Bates. Married 18 June by Rev. Charles
Hopkins. p 285

4 October 1790. Corbin PARRISH and Elizabeth Parrish,
dau. of Alexander Parrish. Sur. John Kellshaw. Wit.
Ann Parrish and Charles Parrish. Married 5 Oct. (Deed
Book 15, p 432). Goochland County Marriage Register
p 279

25 October 1792. David PARRISH and Patsey Thomason, dau.
of Thomas Thomasson. Sur. Archibald Rutherford. Married
25 Oct. (Deed Book 16, p 175). Goochland County
Marriage Register p 281

7 December 1796. David PARRISH and Elizabeth Williams.
Sol[n]. Williams gives consent for Elizabeth. Sur. Dabney
Parrish. Married 8 Dec. by Rev. Charles Hopkins. p 286

9 October 1809. George PARRISH and Susanna Gilliam.
Sur. Willis McKeane. Married by Rev. Conrad Speece.
Recorded 9 October 1810, with a list of other mar-
riages. p 300

17 January 1801. George W. PARRISH and Polly R. Richards, dau. of John Richards. Sur. Charles Lacy. Wit. Richard Bates. Married 23 Jan. by Rev. Lewis Chaudoin. p 289

4 October 1808. James PARRISH and Constance M. Parrish, dau. of Booker Parrish. Sur. John Smith, Jr. Wit. David M. Parrish. p 299

9 August 1815. James PARRISH and Mildred Parrish. Sur. John Parrish. James Parrish is 21 years of age. Married 10 Aug. by Rev. Lewis Chaudoin. p 308

19 October 1807. John PARRISH and Sally Windle. Sur. William Parrish. Wit. Elizabeth Windle and Jane Windle. p 298

6 January 1812. John Fleming PARRISH and Mary Bellamy, dau. of Bradley Bellamy who is surety. Married 6 Jan. by Rev. J. D. Logan. p 303

13 September 1808. John T. PARRISH and Patsey Walker. Sur. Shadrack Walker. p 299

15 February 1802. Jolley S. PARRISH and Rocksey Parrish. Sur. John C. Parrish. Married 16 Feb. by Rev. Richard Pope. p 290

18 December 1786. Meredith PARRISH and Elizabeth Curtis. Sur. Sherwood Parrish. Wit. William Attkisson and Henry Hines. Married 21 Dec. by Rev. Reuben Ford. (Deed Book 15, p 14). Goochland County Marriage Register p 277

26 November 1796. Meredith PARRISH and Molly Layne, widow of John Layne, deceased. Sur. Reuben Saunders. Wit. Micajah Parrish and Mager Parrish. Married 29 Nov. by Rev. Charles Hopkins who says Molly Lane. p 285

29 September 1786. Nathaniel PARRISH and Martha Clarkson. Sur. Anselum Clarkson. Wit. Thomas Meriwether.

31 July 1794. Nicholas PARRISH and Mary Johnson. Sur. Henry Gray. Married 2 August. (Order Book 19, p 674). Goochland County Marriage Register p 283

6 December 1800. Turner PARRISH and Sally Thomasson, dau. of Thomas Thomasson. Sur. David M. Parrish. Wit. Hyllard Thomasson. Married 6 Dec. by Rev. Charles Hopkins. p 289

7 November 1814. Hartwell PARSONS and Margary Kearsey, dau. of George Kearsey. Sur. Garland Kersey. Wit. Woodson Parsons and Augustus Parsons. Hartwell is son of Samuel Parsons. p 307

4 December 1807. Alexander PATTERSON and Polly Jarrott, dau. of Deux Jarratt. Sur. Alexander Jarratt. Married 24 Dec. by Rev. Lewis Chaudoin who says <u>Polly Garratt</u>. p 298

20 August 1790. James PATTERSON and Patsey Sampson. Sur. Stephen Sampson, Jr. p 279

21 August 1790. James PATTERSON and Jane Sampson. (Deed Book 15, p 487). Goochland County Marriage Register p 395

20 September 1802. James PATTERSON and Betsy H. Jarratt, dau. of Dev^x. Jarratt. Sur. Archelus Jarratt. Wit. William Jarratt. Married 23 Sept. by Rev. Lewis Chaudoin. p 291

30 August 1803. John PATTERSON and Elizabeth Attkisson. Judah Attkisson gives consent for Elizabeth. Sur. Major Faudree. Wit. Stephen Clarke. p 292

22 August 1803. Tarlton PATTISON and Joanna W. Jarratt, dau. of Devereux Jarratt who is surety. Wit. Richard Bates. Married 23 Aug. by Rev. Lewis Chaudoin. p 292

4 September 1804. Alexander Spotswood PAYNE and Charlotte Bryce, dau. of Arch^d. Bryce. Sur. John Bryce. Wit. Benjamin Anderson. Married 6 Sept. by Rev. Charles Hopkins. p 293

8 December 1797. Archer PAYNE and Betsy Brooks. Sur. Robert Dandridge. Married 8 Dec. by Rev. Charles Hopkins. p 286

5 February 1810. Archer PAYNE and Lucy Brooks, dau. of Thomas Brooks. Sur. Walker Brooks. Married 30 March by Rev. Lewis Chaudoin. p 300

12 January 1788. Charles F. PAYNE and Polly Adams, dau. of Thomas Adams. Sur. Josias Payne. Wit. Richard Payne. p 278

19 August 1811. Cornelius PAYNE and Sally M. Richardson, dau. of William M. Richardson. Sur. John R. D. Payne. p 302

22 December 1754. George PAYNE, Junr. and Agatha George, dau. of James George. Sur. William Michell. Wit. Randall Holbrook, Josias Payne, Junr. and George Lovell. George is son of Josias Payne. p 265

5 May 1810. John R. D. PAYNE and Susanna Bryce. Arch.
Bryce is her guardian. Sur. John Bryce. Married 9 May
by Rev. J. D. Logan. p 301

21 December 1807. John W. PAYNE and Polly Gilliam, dau.
of John Gilliam. Sur. David P. Cocke. Wit. Preston.
Smith. Married 24 Dec. by Rev. Lewis Chaudoin. p 298

23 August 1755. Josias PAYNE, Junr. and Elizabeth Flem-
ing, (Mrs. Elizabeth Fleming). Sur. Thomas Riddle. Wit.
Thomas Fleming and William Michell. Josias is son of
Josias Payne, Sr. p 265

17 February 1800. Jonathan S. PAYNE and Sarah Pryor,
dau. of William Pryor. Sur. Francis Underwood. p 288

30 April 1773. Matthew PAYNE and Sally Pryor, dau. of
William Pryor. Sur. Samuel Pryor. p 269

22 February 1800. Robert PAYNE and Elizabeth McC. Payne.
Sur. Joseph Shelton. Married 26 Feb. by Rev. Charles
Hopkins. p 288

20 July 1762. Robert PAYNE, Junr. and Ann Burton, dau.
of Robert Burton. Sur. Josias Payne. p 266

14 May 1787. Smith PAYNE and Margaret B. Payne. Sur.
W. N. Woodson. p 277

19 December 1814. Tarlton F. PAYNE and Susan Gilliam,
dau. of John Gilliam. Sur. Nelson Martin. Married 22
Dec. by Rev. Lewis Chaudoin. p 307

16 October 1780. Anderson PEERS and Judith Laprade, dau.
of John Laprade. Sur. Strangeman Hutchins. Wit. John
Laprade, Jr. and Susanna Laprade. p 271

21 October 1793. John M. PEERS and Elizabeth Shields
Vaughan, dau. of Matthew Vaughan. Sur. Reuben Turner.
Wit. John Bass. Thomas Harding is guardian of John M.
Peers. Married 23 Oct. by Rev. William Webber. p 282

4 June 1811. Dr. Thomas PEERS and Sally A. Mayo. Sur.
Isaac Curd. Wit. John Travilian. p 302

24 February 1793. Abished PEMBERTON and Cynthia F. Parrish. (Order Book 19, p 434). Goochland County Marriage Register p 398

14 August 1764. Edmund PENDLETON and Milly Pollard,
dau. of Joseph Pollard. Sur. Jesse Payne. p 267

26 August 1784. Archelaus PERKINS and Ann Michell. Sur.
George Payne. Wit. Fleming Payne. p 273

8 December 1812. Archelaus M. PERKINS, Jun[r]. and Ann D.
Lewis, dau. of Dudley Ragland. Sur. William George, Jr.
Married 10 December by Rev. Lewis Chaudoin. p 304

9 August 1814. Benjamin PERKINS and Mary Nuchols, dau. of
Thomas and Nancy Nuchols. Sur. John G. Childress. p 306

27 May 1761. Constant PERKINS and Mary Allen. Sur.
Bouth Napier. Wit. Jesse Payne. p 266

6 November 1780. Constant PERKINS and Judith Poor, dau.
of Thomas Poor. Sur. John Poor. Wit. Walker Perkins
and William Poor. p 271

10 June 1794. Ezekiel PERKINS and Barsha Ellis, dau. of
Pattey Ellis. Sur. John Crouch. Wit. William Henley.
p 283

10 January 1794. George PERKINS and Frances Peers. Jacob
Woodson, her brother-in-law, makes affadavit that Frances
"is of age and has no guardian". Sur. Ezekiel Perkins.
Wit. Jacob Woodson and John Matthews. Married 23 Jan.
by Rev. Charles Hopkins. (Order Book 19, p 582).
Goochland County Marriage Register p 282

31 March 1813. George PERKINS and Mima Dawson, of age.
Sur. William Lane. Wit. E. Peers. p 305

21 December 1795. Grief PERKINS and Mary R. Michell.
Sur. William M. Richardson. Wit. Arch[s]. Perkins and
Arch[s] Michell. Married 21 Dec. by Rev. Charles Hopkins.
p 284

16 September 1805. Isaac O. PERKINS and Elvira Perkins.
Sur. Nathaniel Perkins. p 294

24 December 1805. James PERKINS and Martha Younger, dau.
of Samuel Younger who is surety. Married 26 Dec. by Rev.
Lewis Chaudoin who says Martha Young. p 295

17 March 1800. Joseph PERKINS, Jr. and Polly Sampson.
Sur. Robert Mosby, Jr. Married 20 March by Rev. Charles
Hopkins. p 288

5 January 1778. Walker PERKINS and Judith Hughes, dau. of
William Hughes who is surety. Wit. William Hughes, Jr.
and Nathan Seems. p 270

23 February 1756. William PERKINS and Susanna Massie,
widow of Thomas Massie. Sur. Benjamin Mitchel. Wit.
Valentine Wood. p 265

5 October 1784. William PERKINS and Judith Clopton, dau.
of Benjamin Clopton. Sur. Edward Martin. Wit. Mary
Clopton and Benjamin M. Clopton. p 273

31 March 1801. William PERKINS and Mildred Bagwell.
Sur. Grief Perkins. Married 4 April by Rev. Charles Hopkins. p 290

19 February 1812. William PHILIPS and Nancy B. Chick,
dau. of William Chick of Hanover County. Sur. Ambler
Chick. Wit. Marcellas Smith, William Dickenson and
John Sizer. Henry H. Dickenson, of Caroline County, is
guardian of William Philips. p 303

19 November 1800. George PHILLIPS and Sally Lovell,
dau. of George Lovell. Sur. Charles Attkisson. Married 22 Nov. by Rev. Charles Hopkins. p 289

16 September 1811. John L. PHILLIPS and Sarah Ragland.
Lewis Turner is her uncle and guardian. Sur. William
Cocke. Charles Terrell is guardian of John L. Phillips.
p 302

18 July 1814. John PHILPOTTS, Jr. and Mary A. S. Quigg.
John Bowles, her guardian, is surety. Married 26 July
by Rev. Lewis Chaudoin who says John Philpots and Mary
Ann S. Quigg. p 306

17 July 1775. Archibald PLEASANTS and Jane Woodson,
dau. of John Woodson, Gent. Sur. John Cheadle. Wit.
Josiah Woodson and Isham Woodson. p 269

7 October 1790. Edward PLEASANTS and Lucy Humber. Sur.
John Humber. Married 9 Oct. (Deed Book 15, p 487).
Goochland County Marriage Register p 279

19 August 1782. Isaac PLEASANTS and Jane Pleasants.
Sur. Arch^d. Pleasants. p 272

25 July 1804. John Thomas PLEASANTS and Anna Maria
Smith, dau. of G. Smith. Sur. Alban Gilpin. Wit.
Sally Pleasants. John Thomas Pleasants is of Powhatan
County. Married 25 July by Rev. Charles Hopkins. p 293

21 April 1772. Joseph PLEASANTS and Mary Guerrant.
Sur. Joseph Woodson. p 268

21 December 1812. Philip S. PLEASANTS and Eliza P.
Pleasants. Sur. Gideon Mims. p 304

16 June 1762. Richard PLEASANTS, Jr. and Anne Leprade, dau. of John Leprade. Sur. Josias Payne, Junr. p 266

15 October 1784. Robert PLEASANTS, Jr. and Elizabeth Randolph, dau. of Thomas M. Randolph. Sur. George Payne. Wit. Matthew Page and Jesse Redd. Robert Pleasants, Jr. is of Henrico County. p 274

30 October 1798. Robert PLEASANTS, Jr. and Elizabeth Clarke, dau. of John Clarke. Sur. Turner Clarke, Jr. p 287

17 December 1812. Robert PLEASANTS and Judith P. Woodson. Sur. John G. Pleasants. Wit. James M. Pleasants and Margaret S. Parsons. Robert Pleasants is of Powhatan County and Edward Mayo, of Powhatan County, is his guardian. Married 17 Dec. by Rev. J. D. Logan. p 304

21 October 1806. Robert L. PLEASANTS and Damaris Pleasants. Sur. Lucius C. Pleasants. p 296

21 February 1775. Archer PLEDGE and Nancey Woodson, dau. of Joseph Woodson. Sur. William Pledge, Junr. Wit. Joseph Woodson, Junr. p 269

14 December 1809. Archer PLEDGE and Elizabeth Garthright, dau. of Absalom Garthwright. Sur. Roderick P. Payne. Wit. Robert Payne and Nancy Woodson. p 300

14 January 1797. William PLEDGE and Polley Pollock, dau. of Margaret Payne. Sur. Rice Graves. Wit. John Pollock. William is "21 years on this date". Married 14 Jan. by Rev. Charles Hopkins. p 286

26 December 1804. William PLEDGE and Mary W. Gray, dau. of Susanna Gray. Sur. Charles Hopkins, Jr. Married 27 Dec. by Rev. Charles Hopkins who says William is son of Archer Pledge. p 293

21 April 1806. James POINDEXTER and Elizabeth Ware, dau. of John Ware. Sur. William Miller. p 296

22 February 1760. Thomas POINDEXTER and Elizabeth Pledge, dau. of William Pledge. Sur. William Robaras. Wit. William Pledge, Junr. and Martha Pledge. Thomas Poindexter gives his own consent. p 266

11 July 1788. Rowling POINTER and Rebecca Walker, dau. of Peter Walker. Sur. William Perkins. Wit. Caty Woodram and Elizabeth Henderson. Rowling Pointer is also written Rolling Pinter. p 278

26 January 1807. Mayer POLLACK and Sisley Barnett, dau. of Hannah F. Barnett. Sur. Elisha Barnett. p 297

15 January 1763. Thomas POLLARD and Sally Harding, dau. of William Harding. Sur. William Meriwether. Wit. George Chowning and George H. Opie. p 267

15 November 1779. Peter POLLOCK and Mary Poor. Sur. Thomas Pollock. p 271

18 March 1811. Abraham POOR and Martha Poor. Sur. Robert Mims. Married 21 Mar. by Rev. Lewis Chaudoin. p 301

2 February 1808. Drury Woodson POOR and Elizabeth M. Britt, dau. of William Britt, Sr. Sur. Francis Underwood. Wit. James Poor and Hannah Britt. Married 4 Feb. by Rev. Lewis Chaudoin. p 298

10 June 1806. Edward H. POOR and Martha Cardin. Sur. Thomas Poor. Married 10 June by Rev. Lewis Chaudoin who says <u>Martha Carden.</u> p 296

21 October 1791. James POOR and Martha Mims. Sur. Robert Poor. Wit. Tar: Bates. p 280

7 February 1787. Robert POOR and Elizabeth Mims, dau. of Lisbeth Mims. Sur. Gideon Mims. p 277

8 March 1785. Thomas POOR and Frances Matthews. Sur. Edward Matthews. p 274

14 February 1786. Thomas POOR and Susanna Haden, dau. of Zachariah Haden. Sur. Robert Haden. p 275

17 September 1771. William POOR and Molly Sampson, dau. of Stephen Sampson. Sur. Stephen Sampson. p 268

15 August 1785. William POORE and Judith Sampson. Sur. William Sampson. Wit. G. Payne. p 274

20 September 1808. Jacquelin A. POPE and Nancy C. Cliborne, dau. of William <u>Clyborne</u>, Senr. Sur. William <u>Cliborne</u>, Jr. Married 22 Sept. by Rev. Lewis Chaudoin who says <u>Jackqueline</u> and spells Nancy's last name, <u>Clyborne.</u> p 299

17 November 1794. Thomas POPE and Christian Johnson. William Johnson gives consent for Christian. Sur. Elisha Leak. Married 20 Nov. by Rev. Hugh French. p 283

16 January 1804. Thomas POPE and Patsey Tuggle, dau. of Henrey Tuggle. Sur. James Tuggle. Wit. Benjamin Anderson. Thomas Pope is a widower. Married 19 Jan. by Rev. Lewis Chaudoin. p 292

14 March 1810. Thomas POPE and Betsey Patterson. Pleasant Attkisson makes affadavit that Betsey is "at least 21 years of age", and he is surety. p 301

2 June 1760. Robert POVALL and Winnefred Miller, dau. of William Miller. Sur. John Miller. Wit. Elizabeth Miller. p 266

6 December 1787. James POWEL and Ursly Tayler, of Chesterfield County. Married by Rev. George Smith, Baptist. Goochland County Ministers' Returns p 313

2 January 1800. William POWELL, Jr. and Polly Graves. Sur. William Miller. Married 6 Feb. by Rev. William Webber. p 288

25 November 1806. William POWELL, Jr. and Mary Riddle. Sur. Daniel Johnson. p 297

16 December 1805. John POWERS and Kitty Owen. Sur.Elisha Leake. p 295

10 August 1808. John W. POWERS and Susanna Sheppard. Sur. Robert Pleasants. p 299

18 December 1782. Lewis POWERS and Patsy Cocke. Sur. Thomas Cocke. Wit. G. Payne. p 27

26 January 1778. Matterson POWERS and Elizabeth Attkerson, dau. of William Attkison. Sur. Josiah Attkinson. Wit. John Brumfield, Thomas Peers, Isaiah Addkinson and Stephen Addkinson. p 270

31 January 1795. William POWERS and Molly Sladyen, dau. of William Sladyen. Sur. William Helms. Married 1 Feb. by Rev. Charles Hopkins who says Molly Slayden. p 283

20 August 1771. Barrett PRICE and Sally Graves, dau. of Ralph Graves, deceased. Sur. John Curd. Barrett was born in April 1749. p 268

31 July 1779. John PRICE and Mary Johnson, whose guardian is Isham Johnson. Sur. David Johnson, Junr. Wit. Walthall Burton, James Johnson, Samuel Price, David Johnson and Benjamin Johnson. p 270

15 March 1784. William PRICE, Jr. and Susanah Cocke.
James Cocke consents. Sur. Thomas Massie, Jr. Wit. G.
Robards, Joseph Lewis and G. Payne. p 273

20 April 1796. George PROFIT and Sally Grubb, dau. of
Daniel Grubb. Sur. Andrew Grubb. p 284

26 December 1807. William PROFIT and Elizabeth Borne,
dau. of Stephen Borne. Sur. William Allen. (See William
Broffit). p 298

6 January 1815. George PROFITT and Mildred Bourne. Sur.
Samuel D. Moss. Wit. James Busby and William Profitt.
Married 7 Jan. by Rev. Lewis Chaudoin. p 307

16 May 1785. Samuel PROFITT and Molly Massie. Sur.
Charles Massie. p 274

8 June 1812. John PROPHETT and Sally Moss, dau. of Samuel Moss. Sur. Dover Moss. Wit. Forest Moss. Married
9 June by Rev. Lewis Chaudoin. p 303

5 November 1783. Abraham PRUETT and Ann Davidson. Sur.
John Jouett, Junr. p 272

11 December 1785. Obey PRUITT and Frances Jarrott.
Sur. Abr^a. Pruitt. p 275

17 March 1794. Obey PRUITT and Nancy Lovell, dau. of
George Lovell. Sur. Harrod Pruitt. Wit. Tar: Bates.
Married 18 March by Rev. Lewis Chaudoin who says Obed.
p 282

22 March 1802. John PRYOR and Sally Smith, dau. of
Robert Smith. Sur. John Woodson. Married 1 Apr. by
Rev. Charles Hopkins. p 291

27 August 1760. Samuel PRYOR and Frances Meriwether,
widow of Nicholas Meriwether, deceased. Sur. William
Meriwether. Wit. John Burnley, Will Pryor and Lawrence Wills. p 266

20 October 1791. Captain Samuel PRYOR and Sally Drumwright, dau. of Thomas Drumwright. Sur. George Drumwright. Married 19 November. (Deed Book 16, p 34).
Goochland County Marriage Register p 280

27 October 1747. William PRYOR and Sarah Wood. Sur.
Valentine Wood. Wit. H. Wood. p 264

16 December 1815. George S. PULLIAM and Lucy S. Diggs,
dau. of Dudley Diggs. Sur. William Diggs "or William
Digges". Wit. Thomas A. Hope. p 308

13 December 1806. Harmon PULLIAM and Keziah Glover. Sur. Robert Pulliam. Wit. John A. Pulliam and Nelson C. Pulliam. p 297

3 May 1811. Nelson C. PULLIAM and Elizabeth W. Digges, dau. of Dudley Diggs. Sur. William Diggs, Jr. Wit. William Digges. p 302

6 August 1811. Thomas W. PULLIAM and Anne Catharine Moore, dau. of Ann C. Moore. Sur. William S. Dandridge. Wit. M. Smith. p 302

21 December 1784. Ellis PURYEAR and Elizabeth Hughes. Sur. Hez^h. Puryear. Wit. John Michie. p 274

20 December 1802. Hezekiah PURYEAR and Eudosia Pleasants, dau. of Joseph Pleasants. Sur. William Cocke. Wit. Reuben Pleasants. p 291

30 November 1795. Hezekiah PURYEAR, Jr. and Jane Laprade, dau. of Susanna Laprade. Sur. James Hughes. Wit. D. Guerrant. Married 3 December by Rev. William Webber. p 284

2 March 1779. Obadiah PURYEAR and Mary Miller, dau. of Mary Miller. Sur. Thomas Miller. Obadiah Puryear is of Hanover County. p 270

12 January 1805. William PURYEAR and Molly Linsy Webber, dau. of William Webber. Sur. Joseph Webber. p 293

2 August 1814. Isaac QUARLES, Jr. and Dice King Pemberton, dau. of Thomas Pemberton. Sur. Asbury Crenshaw. Married 4 Aug. by Rev. J. D. Logan. p 306

5 May 1792. James QUIGG and Patty Jones. Sur. George Payne. Wit. John Redd. p 281

17 September 1784. Isham RAILEY and Susanna Woodson, dau. of John Woodson. Sur. Isham Woodson. Wit. Josiah Woodson and John Cheadle. Isham is of Chesterfield County. p 273

12 December 1786. Thomas RAILEY and Martha Woodson, dau. of John Woodson. Sur. Matthew Pleasants. Wit. William Miller, Josiah Woodson and Philip Woodson. Thomas Railey is of Chesterfield County. Married 20 Dec. (Deed Book 15, p 15). Goochland County Marriage Register p 276

11 December 1780. David M. RANDOLPH and Mary Randolph, dau. of Thomas M. Randolph. Sur. Brett Randolph. Wit. Joseph Woodson. David "was 21 years of age last month". p 271

17 April 1789. William RAYLEY and Judith Woodson. Married 17 Apr. by Rev. William Webber. (Order Book 19, p 328). Goochland County Marriage Register p 394

1 March 1773. John K. READ and Frances Payne, widow of Jesse Payne. Sur. William Pryor. p 269

20 November 1785. Jesse REDD and Mary Woodson. Sur. Matthew Woodson. Married 24 Nov. (Deed Book 15, p 408). Goochland County Marriage Register p 275

18 February 1805. Jesse REDD and Lucy Redford. Sur. W. Miller. Married 21 Feb. by Rev. Charles Hopkins. p 293

27 January 1778. John REDD and Mary Willis, dau. of Ellin^r. Willis. Sur. Pleasant Willis. Wit. John Saunders and William Pierce. p 270

21 July 1762. Edward REDFORD and Ann Curd, dau. of Richard Curd. Sur. Stoakes McCaul. Wit. Richard Oglesby and Edmund Curd. Edward Redford is "21 years of age and upward". p 266

30 November 1808. Jesse E. REDFORD and Elizabeth Shepherd. Samuel Brown gives consent for Elizabeth. Sur. Richard Redford. Wit. John L. Woodson. p 299

16 June 1784. John REDFORD and Ursula Pledge. Sur. William Redford. p 273

19 December 1766. Milner REDFORD and Sarah Lewis, dau. of John Lewis. p 268

19 July 1784. Perrin (Pearin) REDFORD and Susanna Woodson. Sur. Joseph Woodson. p 273

24 February 1802. Richard REDFORD and Sally Woodson, dau. of Joseph Woodson. Sur. Thomas Woodson. Wit. John Bullington. p 290

17 October 1783. William REDFORD and Susannah Ellis. Joseph Woodson, Junr. is Susannah's guardian. Sur. Archer Pledge. William is son of Edward Redford. p 272

4 November 1805. James REYNOLDS and Martha Quigg, widow of James Quigg. Sur. John Philpotts, Jr. Wit. Samuel Branch. Married 6 Nov. by Rev. Charles Hopkins. p 294

30 March 1791. John RICE and Sarah Hopkins. Sur. Charles Hopkins. Married 30 Mar. (Deed Book 15, p 487). Goochland County Marriage Register p 280

28 January 1789. Philip A. RICE and Martha M. Vaughan.
(Deed Book 15, p 286 says Philip A. Rice is of King William County.) Goochland County Marriage Register p 394

7 May 1787. William RICHARDS and Judith Martin. Sur.
William Martin. p 277

15 May 1815. David RICHARDSON and Levinia Thomas.
Thomas Gardner is Levinia's guardian. Sur. Peter King.
p 307

13 November 1766. George RICHARDSON and Elizabeth Miller,
dau. of William Miller, Gent. Sur. Stephen Eubank. Wit.
William H. Miller and Sarah Miller. p 268

8 January 1814. George RICHARDSON and Margaret French.
Sur. Mason French, Jr. p 306

28 October 1793. Giles RICHARDSON and Frances Pace.
Murry Pace gives consent for Frances. Sur. Stephen Pace.
Wit. Charles Amos and Samuel Proffitt. p 282

16 February 1801. Samuel RICHARDSON and Bettey Pettis
Hopkins, dau. of J. Hopkins. Sur. Thomas Quarles. Married 19 Feb. by Rev. Charles Hopkins who says Betty P.
Hopkins. p 290

15 March 1790. William RICHARDSON and Salley Mitchell.
William Mitchell gives consent for Salley. Sur. Arch.
Perkins. Married 18 Mar. (Deed Book 15, p 386). Goochland County Marriage Register p 279

20 December 1784. Archer RIDDLE and Frances Massie. Sur.
James Robards. p 274

20 March 1788. John RIDDLE and Susanna Dawson. (Deed
Book 15, p 240). Goochland County Marriage Register p 394

3 January 1779. Matthew RIDDLE and Jane Crow. Sur. Barrat Farrar. p 270

25 January 1805. Robert RIDDLE and Nancy Johnson. Sur.
Madison Powers. p 293

11 October 1755. Thomas RIDDLE and Agnes Mimes, dau. of
David Mims. Sur. William Robards. Wit. Hezekiah Puryear
and Drury Mims. p 265

11 July 1773. Thomas RIDDLE and Eadith Watkins, "of full
age of one and twenty years", dau. of Benjamin Watkins,
deceased. John Johnson made affadavit as to her age and
he is surety. p 269

22 November 1739. Samuell RIDGWAY and Elizabeth Woodson. Sur. Henry Wood. Wit. Valentine Wood and Christopher Hardwick. p 263

1 July 1742. Samuel RIDGWAY and Mary Bellamy. Sur. Charles Lewis. p 263

23 June 1801. William RIGSBEY and Lucy Adams, dau. of John Addams. Sur. James Adams. William is son of Susannah Rigsbey. Married 24 June by Rev. Richard Pope. p 290

28 December 1803. Samuel RIGSBY and Susanna, (Sukey), Murrer. Sur. William Rigsby. p 292

24 December 1805. Samuel RIGSBY and Ann Thomas, dau. of Charles Thomas. Sur. James Addams. p 295

1 December 1774. James ROBARDS and Mary Massie, dau. of Nathaniel Massie who is surety. Wit. John Robards and Sarah Robards. James, 21 years of age, is son of William Robards. p 269

28 July 1780. John ROBARDS and Ursula Rutherford, dau. of William Rutherford. Sur. John Rutherford. Wit. Molly Rutherford. p 271

24 December 1757. William ROBARDS and Elizabeth Lewis, dau. of Joseph Lewis. Sur. George Payne. Wit. William Lewis, James Cocke and John Lewis. p 265

1 January 1812. Robert ROBERTSON and Sally Dixon, who "is 21 years old". Sur. Jesse Layne. Married 3 Jan. by Rev. Lewis Chaudoin. p 303

10 November 1813. Thomas ROBERTSON and Mary Lewis Cocke. Sur. William Cocke. p 305

15 December 1809. Jessey ROBINETT and Elizabeth Parrish. Sur. Major Parrish. p 300

20 September 1813. David ROBINSON and Mary Hodges, dau. of Jesse Hodges. Sur. Stephen Johnson. Married 23 Sept. by Rev. Lewis Chaudoin. p 305

29 May 1787. Isaac ROBINSON and Elizabeth Wingfield, dau. of Robert Wingfield. Married 30 May by Rev. Reuben Ford who says Isaac Robertson. (Deed Book 15, p 14). Goochland County Marriage Register p 277

3 November 1796. William ROBINSON and Sally Fowler, dau. of Alexander Fowler who is surety. Wit. Fred Bates and Rice Graves. Married 8 Nov. by Rev. Hugh French. p 285

25 September 1805. Charles ROGERS and Huldath Clarke. Sur. John Pollock. p 294

10 June 1801. James ROGERS and Anne Mosby, dau. of Kezia Mosby. Sur. William Mosby. p 290

14 May 1810. Philip ROGERS and Frances Harris. Sur. William Harris. Wit. George W. Watkins. p 301

17 August 1801. Thomas ROGERS and Polly Lovell. Sur. William Foster. p 290

20 January 1792. Samuel ROPER and Marthey Faris, dau. of Sary Faris. Sur. John Bryer. Wit. William Johnson, Thomas Pryer and John Faris. Married 26 Jan. by Rev. William Webber who says Martha Ferris. (Order Book 19, p 328). Goochland County Marriage Register p 281

8 January 1746. William ROUGHTON and Elizabeth Price. Sur. Joseph Price. Wit. H. Wood. p 264

19 February 1786. John (Jack) ROWNTREE and Lucy Gordon, dau. of John Gordon. Sur. John Gordon, her brother. John is son of Randall Rowntree. Married 23 Feb. (Deed Book 15, p 408). Goochland County Marriage Register p 276

21 May 1794. Thomas ROWNTREE and Sally Tinkler. Sur. Samuel Rowntree. p 283

21 May 1796. Thomas ROWNTREE and Sally Sinklur, dau. of Micajah Sinklur. Sur. Samuel Rowntree. Thomas Rowntree, by "consent only". Married 24 May by Rev. William Webber. p 285

15 December 1795. David ROYSTER and Elizabeth A. Sampson, dau. of Richard Sampson. Sur. Thomas Royster. p 284

6 July 1814. Dr. Joseph R. ROYSTER and Eliza P. Tinsley. Sur. Robert French. Wit. George W. Watkins and John H. Royster. Married 8 July by Rev. J. D. Logan. p 306

7 May 1790. William ROYSTER, Jr. and Polly Richardson, dau. of Samuel Richardson. Sur. George Payne. p 279

6 December 1794. Archibald RUTHERFORD and Margaret Parrish, dau. of Booker Parrish. Sur. David Parrish. p 283

31 August 1790. George RUTHERFORD and Lucy Lacy. Sur. Stephen Lacy. p 279

30 June 1797. John RUTHERFORD and Nancy Johnson. Sur. Robert Johnson. Wit. W. Miller. p 286

29 April 1811. Robert RUTHERFORD and Elizabeth Royster, dau. of Thomas Royster, deceased. David Royster is her guardian. Sur. Stephen Nowlin. p 302

10 August 1791. Samuel RUTHERFORD and Anna Parrish, dau. of Booker Parrish. Sur. John Brown. Wit. David Parrish. p 280

11 December 1788. James RYAN and Lucy Alvis. Sur. John Alvis. Wit. John Z. Harris. p 278

19 October 1795. James RYAN and Lucy Green. Sur. Zachariah Alvis. p 284

5 May 1788. Joel RYAN and Lucy Morland. (Deed Book 15, p 240). Goochland County Marriage Register p 394

13 October 1786. John RYAN and Christian Page. Sur. William Page. Wit. G. Payne. p 276

27 May 1812. John RYAN and Sally T. Burgess, dau. of William Burgess. Sur. William Parrish. p 303

7 July 1798. Major RYAN and Mary Page. Sur. John Harris. Wit. James Ryan and Richard Bates. Married 10 July by Rev. Richard Pope. p 287

9 August 1788. Benjamin SADLER and Judith Carter, "the younger", dau. of Judith Carter. Sur. Whitehead Ryan. Wit. Edward Cox. p 278

12 February 1799. Benjamin SADLER and Nancy Logan. Sur. Alexander Logan. Married 12 Feb. by Rev. Charles Hopkins. p 287

21 August 1794. John SADLER and Jane Norril. (Order Book 19, p 674). (See John B. Sadler). Goochland County Marriage Register p 399

18 August 1794. John B. SADLER and Jane Nowel, dau. of Thomas Nowell. Sur. Thomas T. Bates. (See John Sadler). p 283

5 December 1806. Pleasant SADLER and Elizabeth Williams, 21 years of age. Sur. William Williams. p 297

21 August 1753. Abraham SALLEE and Elizabeth Woodson. Sur. John Woodson. Wit. Anthony Christian and Alex^r. Grant. p 264

28 March 1801. William SALMONS and Jane Salmons. Sur. William Salmons, Jr. Married 28 Mar. by Rev. Lewis Chaudoin. p 290

20 October 1791. Stephen SAMPSON, Jr. and Polly Richardson, dau. of George Richardson. Sur. John Richards. Married 22 Oct. (Deed Book 16, p 37). Goochland County Marriage Register p 280

31 May 1787. William SAMPSON and Elizabeth Povall. Sur. Robert Shelton. p 278

18 January 1813. Nelson A. SANDERS and Polly Wooddy Nuckols, dau. of William Nuckols. Sur. Benjamin Cocke, Jr. Wit. Benjamin Nuckols. p 304

13 June 1815. Nelson A. SANDERS and Sarah W. Hughes. Sur. William Hughes. Married by Rev. Reuben Ford who says Nelson Saunders. p 308

6 December 1802. Reuben SANDERS and Elizabeth Aston. Sur. Daniel Aston. Wit. Richard Bates. p 291

21 March 1814. William SANDERS and Frances Nuckols. Sur. Benjamin Cocke, Jr. p 306

1 January 1810. William SANDERSON and Susanna Grubbs, dau. of Matthew Grubbs. Sur. John P. Mundin. Married by Rev. Charles Callaway. Recorded 19 March 1810, in a list of marriages. p 300

23 August 1804, Beverley J. SANDIDGE and Ann E. Hatcher, who "is of full age of 21 years". Sur. William Sandidge. Wit. Kitty Owen. p 293

21 July 1797. John SANGSTER and Agnes Hopper, of age. Sur. John Gammon. Wit. Frederick Bates. Married 24 July by Rev. Lewis Chaudoin who says John Sangston. p 64

15 April 1789. John SASSEEN and Mary Crouch. Married 15 Apr. by Rev. William Webber. (Order Book 19, p 328). Goochland County Marriage Register p 394

7 November 1798. John SATTERWHITE and Jane Ford. Sur. James Satterwhite. Married 10 Nov. by Rev. William Webber. p 287

13 January 1801. Benjamin SAUNDERS and Nancy Wingfield, dau. of Francis Wingfield. Sur. William Webster. Wit. Robert Woodson and John Webster. p 289

1 November 1792. David SAUNDERS and Betsey Page. Sur. John Page. Married 1 Nov. (Deed Book 16, p 147). Goochland County Marriage Register   p 281

12 October 1785. John SAUNDERS and Ann Cauthorn. Sur. James Whitlock.   p 274

17 April 1809. John C. SAUNDERS and Mildred H. Hughes. Sur. William Saunders.   p 299

22 March 1809. Robert H. SAUNDERS and Judith Peers. Sur. William Miller.   p 299

17 January 1810. Robert H. Saunders and Lucy T. Mayo. Sur. Preston Smith.   p 300

15 February 1808. Thomas SAUNDERS and Milly Mims. Sur. Robert Mims. Wit. W. Miller. Married 15 Feb. by Rev. John James who says Thomas Sanders.   p 298

15 June 1783. William SAUNDERS and Sally Crow. Athanasius Barnett is Sally's guardian. Sur. Matthew Vaughan. Wit. William Willis and Anderson Peers.   p 272

10 July 1810. Andrew SCOTT and Lucy Scott. Sur. Samuel Martin. Married by Rev. Lewis Chaudoin. Returned 19 November.   p 301

3 June 1800. Charles SCOTT and Betsy Howell, dau. of Iisac Howell. Judith Howell gives consent for Betsy. Sur. Junior Howell. Wit. Ned Bowman.   p 288

26 November 1751. Daniel SCOTT and Anna Randolph. Sur. John Woodson. Wit. Valentine Wood.   p 264

1 January 1814. James SCOTT and Amey Bennett, daughter-in-law of Isaac Fuzmore, a free man of color. John Lewis'saffadavit states that Isaac Fuzmore, step-father of Amey, gives consent for her mother and himself. Sur. Joshua Scott. Married 6 Jan. by Rev. Lewis Chaudoin.   p 306

8 December 1734. Joseph SCOTT and Sarah Mayo, dau. of William Mayo. Sur. John Barnit. Wit. James Marye and William Allen.   p 263

7 July 1806. Morris SCOTT and Charity Jenkins. Sur. Harris Nichols. Wit. Samuel Branch and J. Smith. Married 8 July by Rev. John James.   p 296

18 October 1799. Riley SCOTT and Nancy Johns. Sur. Joseph Scott. Married 19 Oct. by Rev. Lewis Chaudoin. p 287.

30 October 1787. Robert SCOTT and Tabitha Hopper. Sur. George Payne. p 278

18 November 1793. Henry C. SCRUGGS and Clarasey Herndon, dau. of John Herndon. Sur. Walter Clopton. Married 28 Nov. (Order Book 19, p 674). Goochland County Marriage Register p 282

22 September 1762. James SCRUGGS and Susanna Poor, dau. of Thomas Poor. Sur. Zacharias Williams. p 267

2 March 1787. Littleberry SCRUGGS and Fanny Crenshaw, dau. of Benjamin Crenshaw, Senr. Sur. Benjamin Crenshaw, Jr. p 277

10 February 1810. Benjamin SEAY and Ann Maria McConnel, dau. of Thomas Brooks. Sur. Walker Brooks. Wit. John Dunn. Married by Rev. Lewis Chaudoin. p 300

24 November 1800. Joab SEAY and Susanna Utley. Sur. Reuben Utley. p 289

17 June 1812. Willis SEAY and Betsy Isbell. Benjamin Isbell gives consent for Betsy. Sur. Benjamin Hopkins. Married 18 June by Rev. J. D. Logan who says Willis Sea. p 303

21 November 1808. Peter SHAPARD and Polly Moore. Sur. John W. Powers. p 299

12 March 1788. Richard SHARP, Jr. and Agnes Richardson. Sur. William Miller. Wit. G. Carr. p 278

19 March 1807. William SHELBURN and Susanna Gray, dau. of Susanna Gray. Sur. Stephen Crank. p 297

3 January 1810. James SHELTON and Charity Coons, dau. of Richard Coons. Sur. Edward Fuzmore. Married 4 Jan. by Rev. Lewis Chaudoin. p 300

2 November 1802. James D. SHELTON and Polly Shelton, dau. of John Shelton. Sur. John L. Harris. Married 8 Nov. by Rev. Charles Hopkins. p 291

24 April 1805. Jesse SHELTON and Elizabeth Lacy. Sur. John Shelton. Married by Rev. Charles Hopkins. Returned 25 July. p 294

18 August 1772. John SHELTON and Mary Payne, dau. of George Payne, the elder. Sur. William Lewis. p 268

15 July 1805. John SHELTON, Jr. and Massy Shelton, dau. of Thomas Shelton. Sur. James D. Shelton. Wit. Susannah Chisholme and Polly Chisholme. p 294

13 September 1792. Thomas SHELTON and Milley Atkerson, Louisa. The bond for this marriage is found in Louisa County Marriage Register p 58. (Goochland County Deed Book 16, p 130). Goochland County Marriage Register p 399

19 April 1804. William SHELTON and Nancy Anderson, dau. of Richard Anderson. Sur. Robert Perkins. Wit. John Woodson and Isham Woodson. Married by Rev. Charles Hopkins. p 292

18 January 1813. William SHELTON (Min.) and Maria Coles, dau. of Walter Coles. Sur. John Shelton, Jr. Wit. Robert Mims and William D. Coles. p 305

14 May 1814. Captain William A. SHELTON and Mary Ann Saunders, dau. of Robert Saunders. Sur. John Pollock. Married 26 May by Rev. Lewis Chaudoin. p 306

23 May 1815. Augustine SHEPARD and Ann Johnson, "of lawful age". Sur. John Johnson. Married 25 May by Rev. Lewis Chaudoin who says <u>Austin Shepherd</u>. p 308

8 April 1805. William SHEPARD and Elizabeth Layne, dau. of David Layne. Sur. Lipscomb Crank. Wit. William Glass. p 294

30 September 1815. Anderson SHEPPARD and Martha Farrar. Sur. Peter Sheppard. Married 1 October by Rev. Lewis Chaudoin. p 308

11 December 1812. James SHEPPARD, Jr. and Rachel Johnson, 21 years of age, dau. of Benjamin Johnson. Sur. Jeremiah Pace. Married 11 Dec. by Rev. Lewis Chaudoin. p 304

12 April 1803. Captain David SHIELDS and Nancy Watkins, dau. of Joseph Watkins. Sur. Benjamin P. Watkins. Married 12 Apr. by Rev. Charles Hopkins. p 292

17 December 1781. James SHIELDS, Jr. and Patty Vaughan. Sur. James Vaughan. Wit. G. Payne. p 272

16 July 1796. William SHIPP and Nancy Glass, dau. of John Glass, Sr. Sur. John Glass, Jr. Married 28 July by Rev. Lewis Chaudoin. p 285

19 November 1781. Thomas SHOEMAKER, Jr. and Frances Shepherd, of Henrico County. Thomas Shoemaker, Sr. is Frances' guardian. Sur. Joseph Woodson. Wit. John Lewis and Stephen Crouch. Thomas is the only son of his father, Thomas Shoemaker, Sr. p 271

24 April 1815. William SHOEMAKER and Sarah G. Hicks, dau. of Sarah G. Henderson. Sur. Robert J. Pulliam, Jr. Wit. John Hicks. Married 26 Apr. by Rev. Reuben Ford who says Sarah T. Hicks. p 307

11 September 1788. Archer SHORT and Lavinia C. Wyatt, of Chesterfield County. Married by Rev. George Smith, Baptist Minister. Goochland County Ministers' Returns p 313

20 October 1800. Pleasant SHORT and Dolly Blalock, dau. of Elebeth Blalock. Sur. Jeremiah Blalock. p 288

21 April 1806. Pleasant SHORT and Mary Wade. Sur. Thomas Wade. p 296

21 December 1791. Reuben SHORT and Lydia Clarke, dau. of John Clarke. Sur. Robert Pleasants or Richard Pleasants. Married 22 Dec. by Rev. Reuben Ford. (Order Book 19, pp 327 & 582). Goochland County Marriage Register p 281

31 December 1802. Bernard SIMS (Syms) and Susanah Crenshaw, dau. of Benjamin Crenshaw. Sur. William Isbell. Married 1 January 1803 by Rev. Charles Hopkins who says Bernard Syms. p 291

11 March 1790. Elisha SIMS and Barbara Scott, dau. of Elizabeth Scott. Sur. George Payne. Wit. Major Hancock and Arch. Payne. Married 27 Mar. (Deed Book 15, p 452). Goochland County Marriage Register p 279

27 March 1813. Reubin SIMS and Elizabeth Tate. Each is "of lawful age". Sur. Henry Kersey. p 305

27 December 1792. Zephaniah SIMS and Elizabeth Addams, dau. of George Addams. Sur. John Parrish. p 281

24 May 1814. Robert SINGLETON, Jr. and Susan D. Ragland, dau. of Finch Ragland. Sur. David M. Cardin. Wit. Richard Cocke. p 306

15 December 1800. William SINGLETON and Nancy Hicks, (Nancy Hix), dau. of William Hix. Sur. John Sims. Wit. Fleming Payne. Married 16 Dec. by Rev. Richard Pope who says Nancy Hicks. p 289

11 December 1805. William SINKCLEAR and Nancy Lane.
Sur. Arch^d. Sinkclear. Wit. Thomas Rowntree and John
Willis. p 295

22 March 1800. Dabney SLADYEN and Betsy Bailey. Sur.
Holman Bailey. Married 3 April by Rev. Charles Hopkins.
p 288

16 December 1805. Daniel SLADYEN and Martha Grant, dau.
of Alexander Grant. Sur. John Grant. See Daniel Slayton. p 295

18 March 1813. William D. SLADYEN and Levina Jones.
Sur. William Clarke. p 305

23 May 1796. George SLAUGHTER and Catharine Mitchell.
Sur. John Curd. Wit. Ro: H. Saunders. Married 26 May
by Rev. Charles Hopkins. p 285

24 December 1805. Daniel SLAYTON and Martha Grant.
Married by Rev. Lewis Chaudoin. See Daniel Sladyen.
Goochland County Ministers' Returns p 349

13 December 1785. John SLEDD and Sarah Baughan, dau. of
James Baughan. Sur. Thomas Comer. Wit. John Low and
William Elam. p 275

22 December 1796. Anthony SMITH and Lucy Johnson.
Sur. David Johnson. Married 22 Dec. by Rev. William
Webber. p 286

19 March 1800. George S. SMITH and Eliza Boyce. Sur.
Daniel Boyce. Married 20 Mar. by Rev. Charles Hopkins.
p 288

26 October 1812. Granville SMITH and Mariana L. Pleasants, dau. of James Pleasants, Jr. Sur. John Royster.
Married 27 Oct. by Rev. J. D. Logan. p 304

20 November 1751. Guy SMITH and Anne Hopkins. Sur.
William Pryor. p 264

15 April 1806. John SMITH and Martha Puryear, dau. of
Obadiah Puryear, deceased. Sur. Thomas Eldridge, Jr.
Married 17 Apr. by Rev. Lewis Chaudoin who says John
Smyth. p 296

21 December 1812. John SMITH and Ann O. Payne, dau. of
Tarleton Payne. Sur. Tarlton F. Payne. p 304

23 December 1815. John SMITH and Nancy T. Crutchfield,
dau. of Stephen Crutchfield. Sur. William Crutchfield,
Jr. John is son of James Smith. Married 23 Dec. by
Rev. Lewis Chaudoin who says Nancey F. Crutchfield.
p 308

27 January 1747. John SMITH, Junr. and Elizabeth Hopkins.
Sur. Henry Wood. Wit. Sally Pryor. p 264

18 December 1786. Nathaniel SMITH and Elizabeth Isbell.
Sur. William Isbell. Wit. David England and Stephen Mayo.
Mary Smith gives consent for Nathaniel Smith. p 277

3 January 1803. Noel SMITH and Peggy Scott. Sur. William
Scott. Married 5 Jan. by Rev. Lewis Chaudoin. p 291

17 March 1763. Peyton SMITH and Judith Wadlow, dau. of
Thomas Wadlow. Sur. John Farrar and Robert Cawthon. Wit.
John Laprade and Susannah Laprade. Peyton Smith is of
Henrico County. p 267

7 August 1811. Preston SMITH and Sarah L. Watkins. Sur.
William G. Pendleton. Wit. George W. Watkins. p 302

24 December 1790. Thomas SMITH and Nancy Smith, dau. of
Edward Smith. Sur. Edward Matthews. Wit. Benjamin
Massie. Married 25 Dec. (Deed Book 15, p 488). Gooch-
land County Marriage Register p 279

20 December 1793. Thomas SMITH and Susanna Johnson, dau.
of David Johnson. Sur. James Johnson. Wit. William Attkisson and William Johnson. Married 21 Dec. by Rev.
Charles Hopkins. (Order Book 19, p 582). Goochland County
Marriage Register p 282

4 May 1808. Thomas SMITH and Peggy Boyce. Sur. George S.
Smith. Wit. Preston Smith. Married 5 May by Rev. Lewis
Chaudoin. p 299

27 July 1784. William SMITH and Sarah Payne. Sur. Samuel
Pryor. p 273

20 October 1791. William SMITH and Martha Sampson, dau.
of Stephen Sampson. Sur. Samuel Woodson. Wit. Joseph
Price and William S. Smith. Married 24 Oct. (Deed Book
16, p 37). Goochland County Marriage Register p 280

23 January 1785. John SMITHER and Agathy Payne. Sur.
William George. p 274

1 March 1786. Notley SMOOT and Ann Stratton. Sur. Joseph
Payne. p 276

19 January 1786. George SOUTHWORTH and Elizabeth Barnett,
dau. of William Barnett. Sur. John Barnett. Wit. Thomas
Southworth. p 275

94

19 October 1812. John SPALDIN and Elizabeth Allvys.
Sur. David M. Parrish. Wit. Robert Alvys. John Spaldin
is also written John Spoldin on the bond. Married 2o
Oct. by Rev. John M. Chaudoin who says John Spoldin and
Elizabeth Allvice. p 303

1 January 1803. James SPEARS and Elizabeth Martin, dau.
of John Martin. Sur. Charles F. Bates. Wit. William
George. Married 1 Jan. by Rev. Lewis Chaudoin. p 291

16 December 1805. John SPEARS and Margaret Bates. Sur.
Charles F. Bates. Married 2 January 1806 by Rev. Charles Hopkins. p 295

17 November 1812. Leonard D. SPEARS and Deborah Fowler,
dau. of Alexander Fowler. Sur. Jacob B. Fowler. Married 21 Nov. by Rev. Lewis Chaudoin. p 304

4 July 1786. Isaac STANLEY and Elizabeth Brooks, dau.
of Mayry Brooks. Sur. John Hogan. Wit. Thomas Payne.
Married 4 July by Rev. Reuben Ford. (Deed Book 15, p
14). Goochland County Marriage Register p 276

27 February 1811. Reubin STANLEY and Susanna Hunter,
dau. of Austin Hunter. Sur. Fountain D. Hunter. Wit.
Fr. Underwood. Reubin Stanley is of Fluvanna County.
Married 28 Feb. by Rev. Lewis Chaudoin. p 301

29 October 1784. William STARKE and Elizabeth Kennear.
Each is of age. Sur. Andrew Peers or Anderson Peers.
p 274

21 December 1805. Robert STEPHENS and Susanna Childress, dau. of John and Maden Childress. Sur. Patrick
Childress. Wit. John Childress, Jr. p 295

21 March 1807. Rev. Samuel Sale STEWART and Elizabeth
Smith Dabney, dau. of Cornelius Dabney. Sur. Isaac W.
Dabney. Wit. Lavinia Callis. p 297

17 May 1738. William STITH and Judith Randolph. Sur.
Nicholas Davies. Wit. William Randolph. p 263

21 May 1806. William STONE and Sally Reddy, dau. of
William Reddy. Sur. Benjamin Johnson. Wit. Francis
Underwood. Married 22 May by Rev. Reuben Ford. p 296

20 June 1739. Daniel STONER and Katharine Brooks, dau.
of Peter Brooks. Sur. Thomas Turpin. Wit. H. Wood,
John Hodneth and Michel Brooks. p 263

28 October 1791. Gervas STORRS and Susanna Randolph Pleasants, dau. of James Pleasants. Sur. Isaac W. Pleasants. Wit. Cary Pleasants. p 281

28 October 1805. William A. STRANGE and Mary G. Perkins, dau. of Arch^s. Perkins. Sur. Isaac O. Perkins. p 294

8 December 1787. Peter STRATTON and Mary Netherland Stegar, of Powhatan County. Married by Rev. George Smith, Baptist Minister. The bond for this marriage is in Powhatan County and the above record is in Goochland County Ministers' Returns p 313

3 January 1801. John STREET and Agnes Mims. Sur. Robert Mims. Married 3 Jan. by Rev. Lewis Chaudoin. p 289

25 November 1785. Charles STRONG and Sarah Thompson, dau. of Charles and Elizabeth Johnson. Sur. Charles Johnson. Wit. Isbel Herndon and Susannah Herndon. p 275

6 June 1797. George STRONG and Mary East. Johnson Hodges, who is surety, makes affadavit that Mary is "at least 18 years of age", and George "at least 21 years of age". Married 6 June by Rev. Lewis Chaudoin. p 286

23 December 1799. Mastin STRONG and Nancy East. Sur. Johnson Hodges. Married 26 Dec. by Rev. Lewis Chaudoin who says Masten Strong. p 287

9 March 1791. Sherwood STRONG and Mary Tibbs. Sary Tibbs gives consent for Mary. Sur. Booker Carroll. Married 10 March. (Deed Book 16, p 37). Goochland County Marriage Register p 279

18 February 1796. Jeremiah STROTHER and Martha Payne, dau. of Archer Payne. Sur. Archer Payne, Jr. Married 12 Feb. by Rev. Charles Hopkins. p 284

7 July 1791. John STUART and Susanna Hopkins, dau. of Charles Hopkins. Sur. Thomas Shelton. Married 7 July. (Deed Book 16, p 37). Goochland County Marriage Register p 280

1 April 1786. William SUDDEARTH and Martha Pleasants. Sur. Robert Blanks. p 276

1 September 1800. William SULLIVAN and Rebekah Nowell. Sur. Samuel Noell. Married 2 Sept. by Rev. Lewis Chaudoin. p 288

24 March 1812. Thomas SWIFT and Ann Burch, "21 years of age". Sur. Cornelius D. Chisholm. Wit. Lucy W. Pleasants and William Pleasants. Married 28 Mar. by Rev. W. Cooke. p 303

14 October 1805. Timothy T. SWIFT and Susanna Nuckols, dau. of Pouncey Nuckols who is surety. Wit. Samuel Branch. p 294

9 January 1796. William TAITUM and Polly Layne, sister of Tarlton Layne. Sur. John Layne. p 59

25 May 1811. Elkanah TALLEY and Sally Whitlock. Sur. Benjamin Sadler. Married 30 May by Rev. Lewis Chaudoin. p 110

19 April 1809. Elkaner TALLEY and Rosamond Sadler. Sur. Jesse Sadler. p 104

7 April 1795. Jesse TALLEY and Jane Nelson Askew. Sur. Jedidiah Johnson. Wit. Nathaniel Holland. Married 9 Apr. by Rev. Hugh French. p 56

18 January 1790. John TATE and Susanna Laprade. Sur. John Laprade. Married 18 Jan. (Deed Book 15, p 478). Goochland County Marriage Register p 41

2 January 1815. Nathaniel TATE and Lucy Digges, dau. of John Digges. Sur. Thomas A. Hope. p 123

13 January 1796. William TATUM and Polly Layne. Married by Rev. Lewis Chaudoin. Goochland County Ministers' Returns p 338

18 July 1796. Blagrave TAYLOR and Judith Anderson, dau. of Richard Anderson. Sur. William Fuqua. Wit. John Woodson and Robert Perkins. Married 1 Sept. by Rev. Charles Hopkins. p 60

30 January 1804. Richard TAYLOR and Susanna Hicks, dau. of Meshack Hicks. Sur. John Hicks. Married 30 Jan. by Rev. Lewis Chaudoin. p 87

15 November 1787. William TAYLOR and Mary Stanford, of Chesterfield County. Married by Rev. George Smith, Baptist Minister. The bond for this marriage is in Chesterfield County and the above record is in Goochland County Ministers' Returns p 313

2 October 1792. Richard TERRELL and Lucy Carr. Sur. Samuel Carr. (Deed Book 16, p 130). Goochland County Marriage Register p 48

21 November 1786. Mills TERRY and Sally Lemay. Sur. Sher^d. Parrish. Wit. G. Payne. p 35

10 February 1787. Benjamin THACKER and Anna Grubbs, dau. of Daniel Grubbs. Sur. John Furlong. p 36

21 October 1811. Elisha THACKER and Fanney Coley, dau. of Pege Coley. Sur. Robert T. Barlow. Wit. Elizabeth <u>Coly</u>. Married 24 Oct. by Rev. Lewis Chaudoin. p 111

28 December 1812. Henry THACKER and Catharine Deals, dau. of Jacob Deals. Sur. Lawrence Anderson. Henry Thacker is 21 years of age. p 117

29 January 1788. James THACKER and Mary Faudrie. Sur. Joseph <u>Faudree</u>. p 39

8 September 1813. Thomas W. THACKER and Elizabeth Carrell. Sur. David Carrell. Married 9 Sept. by Rev. Lewis Chaudoin. p 120

17 October 1808. Wyatt THACKER and Frances Johnson. Sur. Jacob Johnson. p 101

27 September 1791. Joel THOMAS and Susannah Parish. Booker Parish gives consent for Susannah. Sur. Bartlet Bowles. p 46

25 August 1810. Meriwether J. THOMAS and Susanna Rigsby, dau. of Susanna Rigsby. Sur. David Rigsby. Wit. Charles Thomas. p 107

22 April 1799. Nathaniel THOMAS and Jenny Mosley, dau. of Joseph Mosley. Sur. James Mosley. Married 22 Apr. by Rev. Lewis Chaudoin who says <u>Janny Moseley</u>. p 71

19 December 1799. Richard THOMAS and Massie Hodges, dau. of William Hodges. Sur. Joseph Atkisson. Wit. Jesse Hodges. Married 26 Dec. by Rev. Lewis Chaudoin. p 73

17 April 1814. Alexander K. THOMPSON and Sarah J. Toler. Sur. John Willis. Wit. Mary Toler. p 121

9 February 1808. William L. THOMPSON and Augusta A. Johnson. Sur. John L. Bragg. Wit. David Johnson. p 99

11 April 1797. David THOMSON and Winnefred Jones Eldridge. Sur. Henry Cox. Wit. Jane Johnson and Judith Cox. Married 13 Apr. by Rev. Charles Hopkins. p 63

23 April 1802. William THURMAN and Nancy Carter, dau. of Susanna Carter. Sur. Robert Powers. p 81

4 February 1795. John THURSTON and Jane Page, dau. of William Page. Sur. William Page, Jr. Married 8 Feb. by Rev. Lewis Chaudoin. p 56

14 March 1799. John D. THURSTON and Polly Barker. Sur. Frederick Layne. Married 16 Mar. by Rev. Lewis Chaudoin. p 70

13 February 1787. Meriwether THURSTON and Elizabeth Lowry, dau. of Matthew Loury. Sur. Matthew Loury, Jr. Wit. Stephin Grainge. Meriwether is son of William Thurston. p 36

9 November 1811. Reuben THURSTON and Frances Page, 21 years of age. Sur. William R. Thurston. Married 21 Nov. by Rev. Lewis Chaudoin. p 112

10 June 1813. William THURSTON and Judith Smith. Sur. William Thurston, Jr. Married 20 June by Rev. Lewis Chaudoin. p 119

7 February 1814. William THURSTON and Polley Walker, dau. of Shadrach Walker. Sur. George Thurston. William is son of John Thurston. Married 9 Feb. by Rev. Lewis Chaudoin. p 121

23 October 1799. William THURSTON, Jr. and Mary Thurston, dau. of John Thurston, Senr. Sur. Meriwether Thurston. Married 24 Oct. by Rev. Lewis Chaudoin. p 72

25 March 1795. John TIBBS and Nancey Muller. Sur. Johnson Hodges. (See John Tibbs). p 56

25 March 1795. John TIBBS and Nancy MULLICE. Married by Rev. Lewis Chaudoin. (See John Tibbs). Goochland County Ministers' Returns p 338

23 December 1797. John TILER and Polly Banks, dau. of Jacob Banks. Sur. Francis Tiler. p 65

24 December 1810. George TILLER and Susanna Layne, dau. of David Layne. Sur. Claborne Layne. Wit. G. W. Watkins. Married 24 Dec. by Rev. Lewis Chaudoin. p 109

15 February 1796. Cornelius TINSLEY and Martha J. Blackwell, dau. of Jesse Blackwell. Sur. Thomas Tinsley. Wit. Stephen Crouch and William Willis. Married 16 Feb. by Rev. William Webber. p 59

17 January 1785. Rives TINSLEY and Nancy Shoemaker. Sur. John Hines. p 31

5 December 1805. Thomas TINSLEY and Sarah Utley, dau. of Obadiah Utley. Sur. Charles F. Jordan. p 91

17 February 1800. William TINSLEY and Sally Wade, dau. of Robert Wade. Sur. Archer Evans. Wit. W. Miller. Married 21 Feb. by Rev. William Webber. p 74

9 March 1764. John TODD and (bond mutilated). Sur. Jesse Payne. Wit. William Ponton and John Marshall. Both are of Cumberland County. John Todd is of Cumberland County. p 267

15 February 1814. Adam J. TOLER and Elizabeth Hubbard. Sur. John Willis. Adam is son of Mary Toler. p 121

17 June 1793. Richard TOLER and Molly Turner, dau. of William Turner who is surety. Married 17 June. (Order Book 19, p 674 says Richard Toler and <u>Mary Turner</u>). Goochland County Marriage Register p 51

17 October 1803. William TOLER and Nancy Toler, dau. of George Toler. Sur. Benjamin Isbell. Wit. John Smith. p 85

14 February 1786. Archer TONEY and Susanna Ennis. Sur. James Tuggle. Wit. Josias Payne, Junr. p 33

22 July 1796. Ely TOLLER and Anney Clarke, dau. of John Clarke. Sur. Philip Lawson. p 60

15 December 1803. Richard TOURMAN and Polley Cocke, dau. of James Cocke. Sur. Robert Powers. Wit. Jin Cocke. p 86

20 October 1777. Thomas TOURMAN and Elizabeth Mitchell, widow of Thomas Mitchell. Sur. John Curd. Wit. Valentine Wood. p 19

21 August 1786. Daniel TRABUE and Elizabeth Farrar. Sur. William Farrar. Married 28 Aug. (Deed Book 15, p 15). Goochland County Marriage Register p 34

1 January 1753. Alexander TRENT and Elizabeth Woodson, dau. of Stephen Woodson, deceased. Charles Bates is Elizabeth's guardian. Sur. John Woodson. Wit. Matthew Woodson and Samuel Branch. p 6

17 May 1799. John TREVILIAN and Mary Watkins. Sur. John Curd. Wit. George Mayo and John Anderson. p 71

13 December 1768. William TRICE and Molly Green, widow of Forrester Green, Jr. Sur. Charles Rice. William Trice is of Amherst County. p 13

24 December 1806. James TRUSLOW and Agnes Mosby Finch. Sur. John Finch. Married 25 Dec. by Rev. Lewis Chaudoin. p 96

8 January 1804. James TUGGLE and Nancy Herndon, dau. of John Herndon. Sur. Jesse Maddox. p 86

18 November 1779. John TUGGLE and Elizabeth Harrison, 21 years of age on the 6th of December, 1779, dau. of Frances Overstreet. Sur. William Ware. Wit. William Harrison. John, "upwards of 21 years of age", is son of Henry Tuggle. p 23

19 December 1791. Thomas TUGGLE and Susanna Herndon. Sur. David Mullins. Married 24 Dec. (Deed Book 16, p 37). Goochland County Marriage Register p 47

21 January 1799. Bartlett TURNER and Nancy Carrell. Sur. Booker Carrell. Married 22 Jan. by Rev. Lewis Chaudoin. p 69

30 March 1789. James TURNER and Patty M. Cosby, dau. of Samuel Cosby. Sur. James Watkins. Wit. Jane Sampson. p 41.

21 September 1812. James TURNER and Mary Pryor, dau. of William Pryor, Sr. Sur. Fountain Duke. p 115

7 December 1808. Nathaniel H. TURNER and Harriot Digges, dau. of Dudley Diggs, Sr. Sur. Thomas A. Hope. Wit. Dudley Diggs, Jr. p 102

11 October 1781. Pleasant TURNER and Agnes Woodson. Sur. Archer Pledge. p 25

18 February 1799. Pleasant TURNER and Polly Carrell, dau. of Nancy Turner. Sur. John Baker. Married 21 Feb. by Rev. Lewis Chaudoin. p 70

7 December 1813. Thomas C. TURNER and Nancy Hunter, dau. of Austin Hunter. Sur. Benjamin Duval. p 120

8 February 1805. William TURNER and Nancy Carrell, dau. of Nancy Turner. Sur. Thomas Strong. Paul Dismukes gives consent for William Turner. Married 9 Feb. by Rev. Lewis Chaudoin. p 89

15 January 1802. Francis TYLER and Sally Scott, of age. Sur. Henry Cockrum. Wit. J. Woodson. Married 18 Feb. by Rev. Lewis Chaudoin. p 80

16 March 1799. Alexander UNDERWOOD and Elizabeth Bibb Harding, dau. of Thomas Harding. Sur. Joseph Puryear. p 70

12 September 1794. Francis UNDERWOOD and Nancy George, dau. of James George. Sur. George Underwood. Wit. Ro. Shelton and A. Campbell. Married 13 Sept. by Rev. Charles Hopkins. p 54

25 January 1797. Francis UNDERWOOD, Jr. and Nancy Drumwright. Sur. John Riddle. Married 27 Jan. by Rev. Lewis
Chaudoin. p 62

30 May 1797. James UNDERWOOD and Frances George, dau. of
James George. Sur. Alexander Underwood. Wit. John L.
Harris and Joseph M. Payne. Married 2 June By Rev. Charles
Hopkins. p 63

13 January 1800. Thomas UNDERWOOD and Elizabeth M. Anderson. Sur. James Underwood. Married 16 Jan. by Rev.
Charles Hopkins. p 74

16 May 1808. William UNDERWOOD and Prudence Royster. Sur.
William Gray. p 100

15 December 1777. John UTLEY and Elizabeth Gordan. Sur.
Joel Ragland. John Utley was born 26 Dec. 1755. Certifi-
cate of age is given by Rev. William Douglas, Minister. p 19

1 October 1803. John UTLEY, Jr. and Ally Chancellor. Sur.
David Utley. p 85

26 December 1795. Obadiah UTLEY and Jane Willis. Married
by Rev. William Webber. Goochland County Ministers' Returns p 339

14 March 1798. Reuben UTLEY and Elizabeth Utley. Sur.
John Utley. p 66

1 February 1781. John VAIDEN and Jenny Moss. Sur. Augustine Eastin. John's name is written John Vaiden or John
Waiden. He is of New Kent County. p 25

12 December 1804. James VAUGHAN and Nancy Pope. Sur.
Thomas Pope. Married 13 Dec. by Rev. Lewis Chaudoin. p 89

26 February 1783. James VAUGHAN, Jr. and Judith Hopkins.
Sur. John Hopkins. p 27

8 December 1806. John VAUGHAN and Ann Childress. Sur.
William Hughes. p 95

11 June 1804. Dr. Nicholas M. VAUGHAN and Anna R. Pleasants, dau. of J. W. Pleasants. Sur. Benjamin Anderson.
Married 13 June by Rev. Charles Hopkins. p 87

21 April 1783. Patrick VAUGHAN and Mary Smith. Sur.
Elijah Brumfield. p 27

5 November 1799. Shadrach VAUGHAN and Sally Howe, dau. of
Thomas Howe. Sur. John Patterson. Wit. Benjamin Davenport. Married 6 Nov. by Rev. William Webber. p 72

12 April 1791. John VINCETT and Molly Green. Sur. William Green. Married 14 April. (Deed Book 15, p 488). Goochland County Marriage Register p 45

5 February 1805. Austin W. WADE and Martha Shields. Sur. Dabney Wade, Jr. p 89

24 January 1800. Benjamin WADE and Elizabeth Green. Sur. Daniel Wade. Wit. Ambrose Wade. Married 26 Jan. by Rev. William Webber. p 74

31 January 1787. Castleton WADE and Judith Chancellor. Sur. Julius Chancellor. Married 1 February. (Deed Book 15, p 15). Goochland County Marriage Register p 36

2 February 1815. Daniel WADE and Ann Bumpass. Sur. William Miller. Wit. Garland L. Bumpass. p 123

28 January 1815. Daniel WADE, Jr. and Mildred S. Dandridge, dau. of Mildred Dandridge. Sur. Archibald B. Dandridge. Married 2 Feb. by Rev. Reuben Ford. p 123

27 January 1813. Peter WADE and Sally R. Pulliam, dau. of William Pulliam. Sur. Thompson W. Pulliam. p 118

9 December 1801. Stephen WADE and Kitty Bibb, dau. of James and Sarah Bibb. Sur. Benjamin Phaup. Stephen is "above the age of 21 years". Married 10 Dec. by Rev. Richard Pope. p 79

21 September 1815. William WADE and Rebecca Woodward, dau. of John Woodward. Sur. Robert J. Robertson. Married 21 Sept. by Rev. Lewis Chaudoin. p 125

24 July 1815. Garland T. WADDY and Patsey Dabney Chisholm, dau. of Thomas Chisholm. Sur. William Thomas. Wit. Charles Colly. Married 27 July by Rev. Reuben Ford. p 125

31 July 1787. George WAKLER and Elizabeth Green. Sur. William Walker. p 37

2 September 1814. James WALKER and Jane McKoy. Sur. Daniel McKoy. p 122

22 July 1789. Joseph WALKER and Susanna Willis, dau. of Ellender Willis. Sur. Zach. Alvis. Wit. William Willis. p 41

8 April 1783. Peter WALKER and Eliner Clarke. Sur. Thomas Hodges. p 27

25 November 1785. Peter WALKER and Elizabeth Ellis. Sur. Richard Johnson. Married 1 December. (Deed Book 15, p 318). Goochland County Marriage Register p 275

16 January 1815. Peter WALKER and Sally Mason, of age, dau. of Elizabeth Mason. Sur. Joseph Gray. Married 26 Jan. by Rev. Lewis Chaudoin. p 123

16 December 1808. Shadrach WALKER and Christian Williams. Sur. John Martin. Married 16 Dec. by Rev. Lewis Chaudoin who says Shadrack Walker. p 102

21 January 1782. Shadrack WALKER and Hannah Shepherd. Sur. Benjamin Johnson. p 26

18 January 1813. William WALKER and Polly Parrish. Sur. Robert Parrish. Wit. George W. Watkins. p 118

18 July 1808. William W. WALKER and Martha Slaydyn, dau. of William Slayden. Sur. John Bevans. Married 21 July by Rev. Lewis Chaudoin. p 101

18 March 1800. Thomas H. WALTON and Betsy J. Richardson, dau. of George Richardson. Sur. William Miller. p 75

18 April 1803. Thomas H. WALTON and Susanna Bates, dau. of Thomas F. Bates. Sur. Charles F. Bates. Married 18 April by Rev. Charles Hopkins who says Susanna W. Bates. p 84

22 January 1790. Hopper WARD and Mourning Ryan. Sur. Larner Bradshaw. Wit. John L. Harris. Married 27 Jan. (Deed Book 15, p 452 says Hopper Warde and Morning Ryan). Goochland County Marriage Register p 41

1 June 1797. John WARD and Lucy Wood. Each is of age. Sur. William Smith. Married 1 June by Rev. Hugh French. p 63

18 June 1798. James WARE and Mary Hudson. Sur. Walter Clopton. Married 21 June by Rev. Charles Hopkins. p 67

25 May 1756. John WARE and Ann Harrison, dau. of Andrew Harrison. Sur. William Pryor. Wit. Nicholas Ware and Bendall Straugham. John is son of James Ware. p 7

4 September 1811. John WARE, Min^r. and Polly Miller. Sur. W. Miller, Jr. Wit. George W. Watkins. p 111

16 December 1793. Joseph WARRENNER and Triphania Turner. William Turner makes affadavit that Triphania is of age. Sur. Elisha Leake. Wit. Tarlton Bates. Married 25 Dec. (Order Book 19, p 582 says Joseph Warriner and Inphana Turner). Goochland County Marriage Register p 52

30 December 1785. Benjamin WATKINS, Jr. and Anna Riddle, dau. of Thomas Riddle. Sur. John Riddle. p 32

22 December 1772. Charles WATKINS and Lucy Curd, dau. of Richard Curd. Sur. Edmund Curd. Wit. John Curd. Charles Watkins is of Henrico County. p 17

3 August 1795. Charles WATKINS and Frankey Massie, dau. of William Massie. Sur. David Glass. Wit. William Massie, Jr. p 57

11 May 1815. George W. WATKINS and Betsy M. Miller. Sur. Marcellus Smith. Married 11 May by Rev. Lewis Chaudoin. p 124

27 May 1790. James WATKINS and Elizabeth Radford. (Deed Book 15, p 478). Goochland County Marriage Register p 399

3 January 1763. John WATKINS and Sarah Turner. Welcome William Hodges makes affadavit that Sarah "is 21 years old or upwards" and he is surety. Wit. William Hodges and James Kennedy. p 10

15 April 1812. John WATKINS and Judith Watkins, dau. of Mayo C. Watkins. Sur. Thomas B. Watkins. Wit. "Mary Watkins signed for Mayo C, Watkins". p 114

12 November 1789. Joseph WATKINS and Sally Perry Johnson. (Deed Book 15, p 478). Goochland County Marriage Register p 395

4 December 1794. Peter WATKINS and Elizabeth McCall, (also McCaul on the bond). Susanna Lacy makes affadavit that Elizabeth is "21 years old and upwards". Sur. Zachariah Alvis. Wit. John Johnson, William Hall, Rebecca Hawthorn, Nancy Lacy and Susanna Lacy. p 55

14 January 1814. Peter WATKINS and Susanna Sanders. Sur. Tarlton Creely. Wit. Salley Saunders. Married 15 Jan. by Rev. Lewis Chaudoin who says Susann Saunders. p 121

27 October 1791. Thomas WATKINS and Violetter Johnson. Sur. Daniel Johnson. Married 29 Oct. by Rev. William Webber who says Violette. (Order Book 19, p 328 says Violette). Goochland County Marriage Register p 46

17 February 1767. William WATSON and Martha Pleasants. Sur. Richard Pleasants. p 12

4 March 1742. George WATWOOD and Mary Taylor. Sur. James Robinson. p 2

23 January 1760. John WAYLES and Elizabeth Skelton, widow of Reuben Skelton. Sur. Martha Wood. p 8

28 September 1807. John WEAVER and Betsy Thomasson. Sur. George Thomasson. (See John Weaver). p 98

28 September 1807. John WEAVER and Betsy Thomas. Married by Rev. Leonard Pope. (See John Weaver). Goochland County Ministers' Returns p 350

13 April 1756. George WEBB, Jr. and Hannah Fleming. Sur. Josias Payne, Jr. p 7

19 February 1785. George WEBB, Junr. and Judith Fleming, dau. of Tarlton Fleming, deceased. Sur. George Payne. Wit. Thomas Mann Randolph. George Webb, Sr. gives consent for George Webb, Junr. p 31

21 October 1799. John WEBBER and Elizabeth Farrar, dau. of Robert Farrar. Sur. Pleasant Turner. Wit. Josiah Woodson. p 72

24 May 1800. Isaac WEBSTER and Ann Scott Pleasants, dau. of James Pleasants. Sur. Robert Cary Pleasants. Married 26 May by Rev. Charles Hopkins. p 75

6 October 1796. William WEBSTER and Susanna Winfield, dau. of Mary Winfield. Sur. Charles Alvis. Wit. John Webster and Nancy Wingfield. p 61

11 December 1797. Benjamin C. WEST and Judith Burnett, dau. of Mary West. Sur. Robert West. Wit. Daniel Porter. Married 14 Dec. by Rev. Richard Pope. p 64

19 May 1782. James WHITLOCK and Susanna Cawthorn. Married by Rev. Reuben Ford. Goochland County Ministers' Returns p 392

12 April 1791. Mitchell WHITLOCK and Cisley Hix. Sur. Thomas Massie, Jr. Mitchell is son of Ann Whitlock. Married 25 April. (Deed Book 16, p 38). Goochland County Marriage Register p 45

22 July 1809. Philip Murrer WHITLOCK and Sally Lowry, 21 years of age. Sur. James Lowry. Married 1 October by Rev. Lewis Chaudoin. p 104

27 September 1792. Thomas WHITLOCK and Hannah Richardson, (Louisa). (Goochland County Deed Book 16, p 130). The bond for this marriage is in Louisa and this record is in Goochland County Marriage Register p 397

4 November 1800. William WILBURN and Tabitha Stovall.
Sur. Josiah Maddox. Married 4 Nov. by Rev. Lewis
Chaudoin. p 76

30 November 1791. Thompson WILBURNE and Betsy Page.
William Page gives consent for Betsy. Sur. James
Clements. Thompson's name is also written Thompson
Wilbon on the bond. p 46

27 December 1815. Henry WILDY and Catharine Whitlock.
Sur. Philip Murrer. Married 27 Dec. by Rev. Lewis
Chaudoin. p 127

13 October 1801. Jesse WILKERSON and Frankey Satterwhite. Sur. Samuel Noell. Married 15 Oct. by Rev.
Charles Hopkins who says Wilkinson. p 79

14 October 1790. Joel WILKERSON and Mildred Pledge.
Sur. William Clarkson. Married 16 Oct. (Deed Book 15,
p 487). Goochland County Marriage Register p 43

19 June 1801. Amos WILKINS and Salley Webber. Sur.
William Webber. Wit. Richard Bates. p 78

16 February 1807. Jesse WILKINSON and Elizabeth Nuckols,
(Betsey). Sur. William Carter. p 97

9 December 1799. Edward WILLIAMS and Susa Utley. Sur.
William Utley. Married 9 Dec. by Rev. William Webber
who says Susanna Utley. p 73

16 December 1777. James WILLIAMS and Elizabeth Mullins,
dau. of John Mullins. Sur. James Page or John Page.
Wit. Daniel Mullins and Jesse Mullins. p 19

20 March 1811. John WILLIAMS and Elizabeth Williams, 21
years of age. Sur. Nelson Hopkins. Wit. Joseph Williams.
p 110

17 October 1796. Powell WILLIAMS and Lucy Woodward.
Sur. Littleberry Bunch. Married 17 Oct. by Rev. William
Webber. (See Powell Williams). p 61

17 October 1796. Powell WILLIAMS and Lucey Woodward,
dau. of Rebekah Hawthorn. Sur. William Hawthorn. Wit.
Littleberry Burch. Powell Williams, by consent only.
(See Powell Williams). p 285

15 October 1798. Samuel WILLIAMS and Jane Utley, dau.
of William Utley. Sur. Powell Williams. Wit. Heziki
Utley and John Williams. p 68

11 February 1778. Solomon WILLIAMS and Lucy Holland.
John Holland is Lucy's guardian. Sur. James Williams.
Wit. Thomas Massie and Anthony Haden. p 20

26 October 1785. William WILLIAMS and Candale Meeks, "of
lawful age". Sur. William Vincent. Wit. Samuel Profit.
p 32

22 June 1798. William WILLIAMS and Mary Lewis, of age.
Sur. John Williams. Wit. Samuel Williams and Hezekiah
Utley. Married 30 June by Rev. William Webber. p 67

21 December 1808. William WILLIAMS and Mary Attkisson,
dau. of Josiah Attkisson. Sur. Thomas Attkisson. Married
22 Dec. by Rev. Lewis Chaudoin. p 103

17 January 1736. John WILLIAMSON and Prudence Cox. Sur.
Charles Turnbull. p 1

13 December 1794. Barttlet WILLIS and Rebecca Faris, 21
years of age. Sur. Lemuel Faris. Wit. John Davenport.
Married 22 Dec. by Rev. William Webber who says **Bartlett**
Willis. p 55

18 December 1788. Edward WILLIS and Susanna Smith. Sur.
George Payne. Wit. John L. Harris. p 40

27 December 1809. John WILLIS and Celey Word (or Sealey).
Sur. Garland Kersey. Wit. William Poindexter. p 105

1 December 1808. Joseph WILLIS and Polly Witt, dau. of
Benjamin Witt. Sur. Samuel Martin. Wit. J. Witt. p 102

10 February 1813. Pleasant WILLIS and Lucy W. Redd, of
lawful age, dau. of Mary Redd. Sur. George Perkins. p 118

17 August 1805. William WILLIS and Susanna Page, dau. of
William Page. Sur. William Miller. p 91

13 February 1793. John WILMERTON and Elizabeth Holman, dau.
of William Holman. Sur. Stephen Johnson. Married 15 Feb.
by Rev. Charles Hopkins. (Order Book 19, p 434). Goochland County Marriage Register p 51

17 December 1792. John WINGFIELD and Milley Clarke, dau.
of Daniel Clarke. Sur. Zacharias Alvis. Wit. William Webster. Married 21 February 1793. (Order Book 19, p 434).
Goochland County Marriage Register p 50

4 October 1803. Joseph WINGFIELD and Lucy Wade, dau. of
Dabney Wade. Sur. Austin M. Wade. Married 6 Oct. by Rev.
Charles Hopkins. p 85

21 January 1812. James WINSTON and Lucy A. Perkins, dau. of William Perkins. Sur. William Perkins, Jr. p 113

28 June 1794. William WINSTON and Elizabeth Shelton, dau. of John Shelton. Sur. John L. Harris. Married 28 June. (Order Book 19, p 595 says Dr. William Winston). Goochland County Marriage Register p 54

6 October 1798. Edward WITT and Ellener Utley, dau. of William Utley. Sur. John Williams. Wit. William Willis. p 68

10 September 1798. Jesse WITT and Betsy Martin, dau. of Samuel Martin. Sur. Benjamin Witt. Wit. Robert Martin. p 68

9 April 1768. William WODLOW and Mary Womack. John Laprade made affadavit that Mary is "above the age of 21 years" and he is surety. Wit. Merth. Price. p 12

21 February 1793. John WOOD and Susanna Ricks. Sur. Gilbert Ricks. Married 21 Feb. (Deed Book 16, p 175). Goochland County Marriage Register p 51

21 December 1793. William WOOD and Marther Carter, dau. of Robert Carter. Sur. Stephen Ellis. Wit. Hezekiah Puryear and Daniel Ellis. Married by Rev. William Webber who says Martha Carter. p 53

31 March 1813. William WOOD and Martha Johnson, dau. of Benjamin Johnson. Sur. John Hughson. p 119

3 December 1789. Benjamin WOODALL and _____ Riddle. Sur. Mathew Riddle. Wit. John L. Harris. Married 12 Dec. (Deed Book 15, p 478 says Benjamin Woodall and Mary Riddle). Goochland County Marriage Register p 41

28 October 1796. Shadrach WOODALL and Nancy Hooker, "about 23 years of age". Sur. William Woodson. Wit. Bouth Woodson. Shadrach's name is also written Shadrick Woodrall on the bond. Married by Rev. William Webber who says Shadrack Woodall. p 61

2 January 1806. John WOODRAM and Elvira Watkins, of age. Mary Watkins "gives consent for Elvira". Sur. William Shelburne, Jr. p 92

7 March 1786. William WOODRAM and Elizabeth Walker. Sur. Isham Clarke. p 33

21 December 1801. Booth WOODSON and Nancy Pryor, dau. of
William Pryor. Sur. Benjamin Bradshaw. Married 23 Dec.
by Rev. Charles Hopkins who says <u>Bouth Woodson</u>. p 79

12 January 1801. Cary WOODSON and Betsy Layne. Sur. John
Layne. Married 15 Jan. by Rev. Lewis Chaudoin. p 77

23 September 1780. Charles WOODSON and Judith Leak, dau.
of Josiah Leak. Sur. George Christian. Wit. Josiah Woodson and Robert Smith. Charles, of Cumberland County, is
son of Drury Woodson. p 24

15 December 1812. Isham R. WOODSON and Sally M. Anderson,
dau. of Thomas M. Anderson. Sur. Joseph Anderson. Wit.
Richard A. Woodson. p 116

17 November 1788. Jacob WOODSON and Polly Woodson. Sur.
William Johnson. p 40

13 June 1791. Jacob WOODSON and Dorothea Peers, dau. of
Anderson Peers. Sur. William Powell. Wit. John Matthews
and Nancy Matthews. Married 27 June by Rev. William Webber who says <u>Dorothy Peers</u>. (Order Book 19, p 328).
Goochland County Marriage Register p 45

10 May 1792. Jacob WOODSON and Molly Gray, dau. of Henry
Gray. Sur. William Johnson. Married 15 May by Rev. Wil-
liam Webber. (Order Book 19, p 328 says <u>Mary Gray</u>).
Goochland County Marriage Register p 48

25 October 1751. John WOODSON and Dorothea Randolph. Sur.
Tarlton Woodson, Junr. p 6

18 March 1760. John WOODSON and Mary Mimms, dau. of David
Mimms. Sur. Charles Christian. p 8

7 November 1808. John WOODSON and Sally Johnson Isbell.
Sur. Christopher Isbell. Married 8 Nov. by Rev. Lewis
Chaudoin. p 101

17 September 1805. John L. WOODSON and Nancy Redford.
Sur. Josiah Woodson. Married 19 Sept. by Rev. Charles
Hopkins. p 91

9 October 1777. John Stephen WOODSON and Anna Woodson,
dau. of Col. John Woodson. Sur. Joseph Woodson. Wit.
Joseph Watkins, Joshua Barner and John Farrar. John
Stephen is son of Matthew Woodson. p 19

4 January 1804. Joseph WOODSON and Betsy Parrish. Sur.
Lewis Hunter. Wit. Benjamin Cocke, Jr. Joseph is son of
Jacob Woodson. p 86

30 December 1769. Joseph WOODSON, Jun[r]. and Mildred Redford, dau. of William Redford, deceased. Stokes McCaul is Mildred's guardian. Sur. David Maddox. Joseph, Jun[r]. is son of Joseph Woodson. p 14

22 November 1778. Josiah WOODSON and Elizabeth Woodson, dau. of Matthew Woodson. Sur. Lucy Wood. Wit. Thomas Harding and William McCaul. Josiah is son of John Woodson. p 21

2 October 1815. Matthew WOODSON and Paulina Woodson, dau. of Philip Woodson. Sur. Tarlton Woodson. p 125

24 October 1806. Milner WOODSON and Nancy Johnson, dau. of William Johnson. Sur. Joseph Woodson, Jr. p 95

30 September 1790. Philip WOODSON and Salley Woodson, dau. of Dorothea Woodson. Sur. Arch[d]. Pleasants. Married 3 October by Rev. William Webber. (Order Book 19, p 328). Goochland County Marriage Register p 43

27 November 1811. Richard A. WOODSON and Susan H. Royster, dau. of Mary Royster who is her guardian. Sur. William Blunkall. Wit. John Woodson. p 112

30 January 1804. Robert WOODSON and Elizabeth Pledge. Sur. William Harris. p 87

16 June 1777. Samuel WOODSON and Elizabeth Payne, dau. of George Payne, Sr. Sur. Nathaniel G. Morris. p 19

11 June 1812. Samuel WOODSON and Sally Johnson, dau. of William Johnson. Sur. Milner Woodson. Wit. Polly Maddox. Married 11 June by Rev. Lewis Chaudoin. p 115

9 August 1789. Stephen WOODSON and Sarah Crouch. (Deed Book 15, p 318). Goochland County Marriage Register p 394

11 November 1811. Stephen WOODSON and Polly Hatcher. Sur. Frank W. Redford. p 112

15 February 1796. Thomas WOODSON and Sally Saunders, of lawful age, niece of Robert H. Saunders who is surety. Married 28 Feb. by Rev. William Webber. p 60

23 March 1741. Tucker WOODSON and Sarah Hughes, dau. of Robert Hughes. Sur. John Cannon. Wit. John Woodson. Stephen Woodson is guardian of Tucker. p 2

19 November 1798. William WOODSON and Judith H. Cocke. Sur. James Cocke. p 68

27 January 1792. Benjamin WOODWARD and Sally Gray, dau. of Henry Gray. Sur. George Payne. Married 20 Jan. by Rev. William Webber. (Order Book 19, p 328). Goochland County Marriage Register p 47

25 December 1809. Jeremiah WOODWARD and Frankey M. Pledge. Sur. William Miller. Married 26 Dec. by Rev. Lewis Chaudoin. p 105

4 February 1790. John WOODWARD and Jane Ellis. (Deed Book 15, p 386). Goochland County Marriage Register p 395

11 December 1795. Joshua WOODWARD and Lucy Gray, dau. of Henry Gray. Sur. Jacob Woodson. (See Joshua Woodward). p 58

12 December 1795. Joshua WOODWARD and Lucy Dixon. Married by Rev. William Webber. (See Joshua Woodward). Goochland County Ministers' Returns p 339

28 December 1802. Nathaniel WOODWARD and Elizabeth Puryear, dau. of Ann Puryear. Sur. William Pledge. p 83

20 September 1799. Jeremiah WOOLRIDGE and Susanna Farrar, dau. of William Farrar. Sur. Tene Hancock. Married 3 Oct. by Rev. William Webber. p. 72

10 February 1790. Archer WORSHAM and Nancy --ith. Sur. Alexander Fowler, Jr. Married 11 Feb. (Deed Book 15, p 478 says Nancy Smith). Goochland County Marriage Register p 41

19 December 1806. William R. WRIGHT and Sarah Alvis. Sur. John Bush. Wit. P. Smith and Rod. P. Payne. Married 20 Dec. by Rev. Lewis Chaudoin. p 96

6 December 1796. Richard WYATT and Nancy Ware, dau. of John Ware. Sur. R. W. Peatross. Married 8 Dec. by Rev. Charles Hopkins. p 62

21 October 1762. John YARBROUGH and Barshaba Harris, dau. of William Harris. Sur. William Meriwether. Wit. William Spurlock and Fanney Yarbrough. John is son of Thomas Griggs Yarbrough. p 10

20 January 1802. Pleasant YOUNGHUSBAND and Mrs. Elizabeth Pleasants. Sur. Isaac W. Pleasants. Married 20 March by Rev. Charles Hopkins. p 80

I N D E X T O B R I D E S

___?___ ___?___		12
_____, Molley		30
--gatt, Nancy		22
--ith, Nancy		111
Mutilated Bond		99

A

Adams, Elizabeth		17
Lucy		84
Martha		1
Milly		57
Polly		73
Addams, Elizabeth		91
Allen, Martha		13
Mary	33,	75
Allvice, Elizabeth		94
Allvys, Elizabeth		94
Alvice, Nancy		1
Alvis, Agnes		16
Elizabeth		71
Lucy	19,	86
Nancy		1
Patsy		2
Polly	12,	70
Sarah		111
Anderson, Betsy		47
Elizabeth M.		101
Jane		31
Judith		96
Lucy - (2)		4
Lucy B.		42
Nancy		90
Rhoda		45
Sally M.		109
Susanna		2
Argyle,Rebecca	59,	60
Arne, Elizabeth		10
Ascue, Frances		33
Ashbrook, Elizabeth		5
Ashurst, Mary		29
Askew, Jane Nelson		96
Rebecca		27
Asque, Rebekah		27
Aston, Elizabeth		87
Ellinor		58
Atkerson, Milley		90
Atkins, Polly		29

Atkison, Nancy	10
Attkerson, Elizabeth	79
Attkins, Jane	34
Attkison, Frances	3
Jane	34
Attkisson, Elizabeth	73
Elizabeth Ann	59
Frances	44
Judith	33
Maria	15
Mary	107
Milly	15
Nancy	13
Patsey	28
Sally	37
Austin, Dosha	23
Peggy	58

B

Bagwell, Mildred		76
Bailey, Agnes		54
Betsy		92
Martha		30
Baker, Betsey		36
Elizabeth E.		36
Hannah		65
Banks, Elizabeth		28
Jane		1
Judith		23
Mary		45
Nancy		19
Polly	19,	98
Sally		56
Barker, Judith		52
Polly		98
Barnett, Elizabeth		93
Nancy		68
Polly		49
Sisley		78
Bassett, Fanny		14
Bates, Anna		46
Hannah		26
Margaret		94
Mary H.		15
Susanna		103
Susanna W.		103
Baugh, Polly		40

Baughan, Sarah	92
Baughn, Anne	47
Bellamy, Mary	72, 84
Precilla	5
Bennett, Amey	88
Bernard, Mary	28
Susanna C.	55
Bibb, Elizabeth	28
Kitty	102
Susanna	16
Binford, Elizabeth A.	17
Binns, Suckey	18
Blackwell, Jane	11
Martha J.	98
Blalock, Dolly	91
Mourning	26
Blankenship, Nancy	10
Blunakall, Polly	57
Boles, Marget	21
Bolling, Ann	54
Jane S.	29
Borne, Elizabeth	80
Bourne, Mildred	80
Bowdry, Elizabeth	7
Bowen, Blendena	31
Bowles, Elizabeth P.	9
Marget	21
Martha	31
Mary	58
Nancey	47
Nancy	11
Salley	33
Boyce, Eliza	92
Peggy	93
Sarah 12(2),	20
Bradley, Elizabeth	36
Bradshaw, Ann	9
Elizabeth	59
Mary	9
Nancy	52
Brag, Sarah	47
Bride, Elizabeth M.	5
Brill, Elizabeth	61
Britt, Elizabeth	61
Elizabeth M.	78
Hannah	39
Jane	63
Martha	21
Mary	49
Susanna	39
Broaddus, Jane C.	10
Brooks, Betsy	73

Brooks, Elizabeth	94
Katharine	94
Lucy	73
Brown, Caty	20
Martha	50
Nancy	49
Susannah	36
Bruce, Sarah	43
Brumfield, Caty	20
Bryce, Charlotte	73
Elizabeth	30
Mary G.	55
Susanna	74
Bullock, Nancy	39
Bumpass, Ann	102
Burch, Ann	95
Sarah	48
Burgess, Sally T.	86
Burnett, Judith	105
Burnley, Mrs. Harriet T.	67
Burton, Ann	74
C	
Cannon, Martha	71
Carden, Elizabeth	10, 63
Judith	27
Carder, Mary	42
Cardin, Elizabeth	10, 63
Martha	78
Mary	42
Patsy	44
Carr, Lucy	96
Carrell, Elizabeth	97
Joanna	7
Nancy (2)	100
Polly	100
Salley	13
Carrol, Jane	7
Carter, Elizabeth	9
Judith,"the	
younger"	86
Martha 47, 108	
Marther	108
Nancy	97
Patsey	25
Cary, Polly M.	68
Causby, Mary	9
Cauthorn, Ann	88
Chancellor, Ally	101
Betsy	19
Judith	102

Chastain, Mary Anne	17	
Cawthorn, Susanna	105	
Cheatham, Polly	34	
Cheattum, Betsy	66	
Cheatum, Kitty	40	
Chichester, Mary	4	
Chick, Nancy B.	76	
Patsey Seldon	50	
Childress, Ann	101	
Elizabeth	68	
Jane	7	
Susanna	94	
Chisholm, Catharine	33	
Mary A.	20	
Patsey Dabney	102	
Chrismas, Polly	37	
Christian, Frances	14	
Clark, Mary	31	
Clarke, Anney	99	
Eliner	102	
Elizabeth	2, 77	
Huldath	85	
Jane E.	49	
Jeny	59	
Keturah	34	
Lydia	91	
Milley	107	
Nancy	52	
Patsey	41	
Susanna	67	
Thursa	14	
Thursey	14	
Winifred	1	
Clarkson, Martha	72	
Mary	39	
Clearke, Jenny	59	
Clements, Elizabeth	69	
Elizabeth O.	31	
Jane C.	51	
Nancy	1, 43	
Polly M.	33	
Cliborne, Nancy C.	78	
Clopton, Judith	76	
Mary	44	
Susaa	41	
Clyborne, Nancy C.	78	
Cock, Peggey Meredith	16	
Cocke, Anne	43	
Elizabeth	40, 66	
Elizabeth P.	8	
Jane	54	
Judith H.	110	
Martha	8	
Cocke, Mary	61	
Mary Lewis	84	
Nancy P.	32	
Patsy	79	
Peggy Meridith	16	
Phebe	49	
Polley	99	
Polly	39	
Susanah	80	
Cockran, Elizabeth	42	
Polly	18	
Ruth	18	
Cockrane, Eliza.	28	
Cogil, Sally	24	
Cole, Mary	4	
Coleman, Betsey	54	
Coles, Maria	90	
Coley, Fanney	97	
Comer, Ann	2	
Nancy	22	
Coons, Charity	89	
Cooper, Nancey	57	
Nancy	18	
Patsey	20	
Rachel	12	
Cosby, Betsy	62	
Patty M.	100	
Cousins, Abbey	61	
Chloe	19	
Cox, Ann	3	
Judith	1	
Prudence	107	
Craddock, Anne	52	
Crafton, Elizabeth	24, 25	
Mary	52	
Cragwall, Betsy	16	
Elizabeth Ann	16	
Crank, Mrs. Elizabeth	67	
Crenshaw, Fanny	89	
Martha	3	
Nancy	25, 39	
Susannah	91	
Crouch, Mary	87	
Sally	16	
Sarah	110	
Susanna	67	
Crow, Jane	83	
Sally	88	
Crowdas, Mary	30	
Crutchfield, Elizabeth	4, 12	
Nancey F.	92	
Nancy T.	92	

Crutchfield, Polly 56
    Sally 56
Curd, Ann 82
    Ann T. 37
    Elizabeth 68
    Fanny 53
    Lucy 104
    Nancy W. 21
    Rebecca 2
Curtis, Elizabeth 72

D

Dabney, Elizabeth G. 48
    Elizabeth Smith 94
    Mary 35
    Polly A. 24
Dandridge, Dorothea Ann 45
    Elizabeth T. 22
    Jane 55
    Martha Hale 29
    Mildred S. 102
Daniel, Betsy 35
    Mary 41
    Sally 7
Davidson, Ann 80
Davis, Elizabeth 31
Dawson, Mima 75
    Susanna 83
Deals, Catharine 97
Demue, Nancy 19
Demure, Milley 25
Denton, Polly 48
Depriest, Jane 14
Digges, Elizabeth W. 81
    Harriot 100
    Lucy 96
Diggs, Lucy S. 80
Dimue, Polly 69
Dinue, Polly 69
Dixon, Lucy 111
    Sally 84
Dobbins, Jane 46
Douglass, Margaret 62
Dowdy, Elizabeth 53
    Frances 53
    Sarah 13
Drake, Lydia 69
Drumwright, Nancy 101
    Polly 57
    Sally 80
Dudley, Judith 23

Duke, Mary Johnson 24
    Nancy J. 24
    Unity 24
Dupriest, Jane 14

E

East, Ann 26
    Betsy 13
    Mary 95
    Nancy 95
Eldridge, Jane 47
    Judith 19
    Sarah 39
    Winnefred Jones 97
Ellis, Barsha 75
    Elizabeth 103
    Jane 111
    Lucy 3
    Nancey 27
    Sarah 41
    Susanna 55
    Susanna D. 9
    Susannah 82
Ennis, Susanna 99

F

Fagg, Marian 16
    Mary Ann 16
Faris, Marthey 85
    Nancy 64
    Rebecca 107
Farish, Katcread 52
Farmer, Betsy 66
    Elizabeth 66
Farrar, Ann 64
    Elizabeth 5, 99, 105
    Lucy 21, 44
    Martha 90
    Mary Ann 46
    Polly 36
    Sally 30
    Sarah 28
    Susanna 111
Faudree, Frances 56
    Jane 21
    Margaret 15
Faudrie, Mary 97
Ferris, Martha 85
Finch, Agnes Mosby 99
Fleming, Elizabeth 74

Fleming, Mrs. Elizabeth,74
    Hannah   105
    Judith   105
    Mary   6
Ford, Betsy   38
    Elizabeth B.   28
    Fanny   65
    Jane   87
    Lucy   27
    Mary   26
    Nancy   51
    Sally   29
    Sarah   41
Forster, Christian   18
Foster, Nancy   51
Fowler, Deborah   94
    Magdalene   7
    Magdaline   11
    Mary S.   61
    Sally   85
Fox, Ann   11
French, Ann M.   38
    Elizabeth   43
    Margaret   83
Fulcher, Charlotte   61
Furlong, Elizabeth   34

G

Garratt, Polly   73
Garthright, Elizabeth 77
Gay, Sally   29
Gennatt, Polly   25
George, Agatha   73
    Anne   32
    Frances   101
    Mary   18
    Nancy   57, 100
    Susannah   41
Gilbert, Sicily   6
Gill, Ritta   69
Gilliam, Agnes   17
    Constance P.   67
    Constantine P.   67
    Elizabeth   17
    Martha T.   71
    Mary   58
    Polly   74
    Salley   52
    Susan   74
    Susanna   71
Glass, Catharine   43
    Frances   12

Glass, Nancy   90
    Sally   52
Glover, Keziah   81
Going, Agnes   68
Goode, Mary   61
Gordan, Elizabeth 101
Gordon, Ann S.   11
    Fanny   55
    Judith   55
    Lucy   85
    Mary   28
    Nancy   55
Grant, Jane   34
    Martha - (2)   92
Graves, Charlotte   57
    Elizabeth   40
    Lucy   1
    Martha   68
    Polly   79
    Sally   79
Gray, Elizabeth M. 15
    Jane   31
    Jane M.   31
    Jo Anne   56
    Lucy   111
    Mary W.   77
    Molly   109
    Sally   111
    Susanna   89
Green, Anne   59
    Elizabeth - (2) 102
    Frances   27
    Frankey   27
    Lucy   28, 86
    Molly   99, 102
    Peggy   2
    Savara   15
Gresham, Jane   25
Groomes, Polly H. 71
Grubb, Nafanar   15
    Sally   80
Grubbs, Anna   96
    Patsey   2
    Susanna   87
Guerrant, Elizabeth 62
    Jane   34
    Janey   34
    Jenney   34
    Mary   76
Guinn, Aggy   18

118

H

Haden, Elizabeth	66
Susanna	78
Halbird, Nancy	62
Hall, Ann	23
Elizabeth	20
Mary	62
Nancy	23
Halsall, Elizabeth	50
Hancock, Elizabeth	69
Martha - (2)	3
Polly	70
Sarah	64, 70
Susanna	64
Hancocke, Judah	2
Hardin, Judith	32
Harding, Elizabeth Bibb	100
Sally	70, 78
Harris, Aggey	1
Barshaba	111
Elizabeth	29, 39
Frances	85
Sarah - (2)	28
Harrison, Ann	103
Elizabeth	100
Hashaw, Polly	18
Hatcher, Ann E.	87
Ann Elizabeth	21
Elizabeth P.	53
Polly	110
Helms, Polly	24
Henderson, Betsy	62
Elizabeth	62
Herndon, Catey	39
Clarasey	89
Isbell	11
Nancy	99
Rosanna	66
Susanna	100
Hicks, Mary	6
Nancy	13, 91
Sarah G.	91
Sarah T.	91
Susanna	96
Higgason, Huldah	39
Nancy	1
Hines, Martha	46
Hix, Alsey	60
Cisley	105
Nancy	91

Hodges, Christian	70
Elizabeth	56
Jane	1
Lucy	6
Martha	69
Mary	11, 84
Massie	97
Nancy	56, 70
Patsy	69
Sarah	50
Susanna	2
Holland, Harriet	17
Lucy	107
Mary	12
Matilda	41
Nancy	44
Patsey	5
Polley B.	51
Sally	41
Susanna, 27, 48, 53, 60
Holman, Elizabeth	107
Peggy M.	38
Peggyan	38
Polly W.	62
Sally	42
Hooker, Nancy	108
Polley	31
Sarah	67
Hopkins, Anne	92
Bettey Pettus	83
Betty P.	83
Elizabeth	93
Judith	101
Mary	12
Molley	31
Sarah	82
Susanna	95
Hopper, Agnes	87
Elizabeth	68
Milley	70
Tabitha	3, 89
Houchins, Lucy	2
Howard, Mary	36
Howe, Sally	101
Howell, Betsy	10, 88
Betsy Ann	4
Judith	45
Hubbard, Elizabeth	99
Hudson, Mary	103
Hughes, Elizabeth	81
Judith	75
Mildred H.	88

Hughes, Nancy 30
   Polly 5
   Sarah 110
   Sarah W. 87
Hughson, Susan H. 47
Humber, Christian 46
   Elizabeth 58
   Judith 19
   Lucy 76
Hume, Charlotte 38
Hunter, Nancy 100
   Susanna 94

I

Isaacs, Nancy 59
Isbell, Ann 61
   Betsy 89
   Elizabeth 93
   Polly 61
   Sally Johnson 109

J

Jackson, Lucy P. 8
James, Maudlin 65
   Nancy 40
   Polly 53
Jarratt, Betsy H. 73
   Elizabeth C. 16
   Jane 7
   Joanna W. 73
   Judith 49
   Polly 73
   Susanna 7, (2)- 20
   Susannah 20
Jarrett, Martha 42
Jarrott, Frances 80
Jenkins, Charity 88
   Judith 59
   Sally 46
Jennings, Nancy 65
Johns, Nancy 88
   Salley 18
   Susanna 64
Johnson, Agnes 5
   Alcey 60
   Alice 60
   Ann 90
   Anna 47
   Augusta A. 97
   Betsy 51
   Christian 58, 78

Johnson, Ealsey 60
   Elizabeth 39
   Frances 97
   Hannah 44
   Jane 44, 58
   Johannah 66
   Judith 36
   Judith J. 42
   Lucy 92
   Martha 108
   Mary 10, 44, 58, 72, 79
   Molly 32, 47
   Nancy 20, 38, (2)-48, 86, 110
   Patsey 57
   Polly 37
   Rachel 90
   Rebecca 15
   Sally 9, 15, 110
   Sally Perry 104
   Sophia 8
   Susanna 64, 66, 93
   Susannah 69
   Violette 104
   Violetter 104
Jones, Eliza 59
   Elizabeth 8
   Jane 16
   Levina 92
   Mary 43
   Patty 81
   Susanna 53
Jordan, Milley 38
   Patsy 26
   Sally 62
   Sarah 12, 26
   Susannah 65

K

Kannon, Mary 37
Kearsey, Margary 72
Kelly, Sally 8
Kennear, Elizabeth 94
Kerr, Ann Poindexter 45

L

Lacy, Dorothea 34
   Elizabeth 48, 89
   Lucy 85
   Nancy 4

Lacy, Polly 35
    Susanna 32
Laforce, Judith 12
Lane, Molly 72
    Nancy 92
Lang, Ann 17
Laprade, Betsey 34
    Elizabeth 6
    Jane 81
    Johanna 63
    Judith 74
    Martha 37
    Susanna 96
Lawrence, Nancy 48
    Polly C. 51, 56
Layne, Betsy 109
    Clarissa 33
    Elizabeth 90
    Elizabeth W. (2)-52
    Lucy 59
    Molly 8, 72
    Nancy 19, 21
    Polly 96
    Roxey Ann 66
    Roxy Ann 61
    Salley 49
    Susanna 98
Leak, Judith 109
Leake, Kitty 69
    Lucy 49
Lee, Harriott 57
    Mary 31
Leforce, ___?___ 14
LeMay, Mary Magdaline 63
Lemay, Sally 96
    Susanna 46
Leprade, Anne 77
Lewis, Ann - (2) 65
    Ann D. 75
    Betsey 54
    Elizabeth 35, 51, 84
    Frances 55
    Jane 22
    Martha 18
    Mary 3, 107
    Mary H. 54
    Nancy 36
    Sarah 58, 82
Linch. Nancy 2
Logan, Julia 57
    Nancy 86
Loury, Keturah 46

Lovell, Nancy 80
    Polly 85
    Sally 76
    Sophia 42
    Susanna 8
Lowry, Caty 46
    Elizabeth 98
    Nancy 57
    Sally 105
Lynch, Nancy 4

Mc

McBride, Ann 9
    Betsey 6
    Elizabeth 6
McCall, Elizabeth 104
McCaul, Elizabeth 104
    Mary 36
    Sally 27
McConnel, Ann Maria 89
McDonald, Elizabeth P. 64
McKoy, Jane 102

M

Maddocks, Elizabeth 22
Maddox, Mary 58
    Sally 31
Madocks, Catherine 48
Mallory, Judith 58
    Mourning T. 65
    Sally B. 11
Mann, Sally 55
Mantlo, Mary 47
Martin, Betsy 108
    Elizabeth 94
    Judith 83
    Nancy 4, 57
    Patsy 63
    Polly 45, 53, 59
    Rhoda 31
    Sarah 50
    Susanna 58
Mason, Sally 103
Massie, Agnes 53
    Ann 63
    Betsey 32
    Constance 63
    Elizabeth 60
    Frances 83
    Frankey 104

Massie, Martha	63	Mitchell, Polly	23
Mary	84	Salley	83
Molly	80	Susanna	69
Nancy	32	Moody, Mary	4
Rebekah	63	Moore, Anne Catharine	81
Mrs. Sally	10	Eliza	22
Salley M.	43	Judith	59
Susanna	76	Patsy	28
Matthews, Frances	78	Polly	89
Jane	40	Moreland, Elizabeth	39
Jane W.	23	Morland, Lucy	86
Polley P.	4	Morris, Sarah	51
Polly	43	Morrison, Jane	50
Sarah B.	5	Morrissette, Elizabeth	14
Mayo, Jane L.	38		46
Lucy T.	88	Margarett	28
Mary	33	Margrete	28
Sally A.	74	Morse, Ann	24
Sarah	88	Morton, Rebecca	26
Meanly, Hannah	41	Mosby, Anne	85
Susanna	41	Moseley, Janny	97
Meeks, Candale	107	Mosley, Febus	22
Merin, Mary	44	Jenny	97
Meriwether, Frances	80	Moss, Cicily	7
Martha	61	Frances	57
Michell, Ann	75	Jenny	101
Mary R.	75	Sally	80
Molly		Muller, Nancey	98
Michie, Polly	60	Mulles, Elizabeth	40
Miller, Betsy M.	104	Mullice, Nancy	98
Elizabeth	35, 83	Mullins, Ann	8
Margaret	38	Elizabeth	106
Mary	81	Frances	27
Mary H.	5	Patsey	10
Mary Heath	5, 30	Mullis, Polly	36
Polly	103	Murrel, Martha	28
Sarah	41	Murrer, Sukey	84
Susanna	26	Susanna	84
Winnefred	79	Muse, Delphia	43
Mimes, Agnes	83		
Mimms, Mary	109	**N**	
Mims, Agnes	40, 95		
Ann	15	Napier, Ann F.	11
Deborah	43	Elizabeth	9
Elizabeth	78	Neaves, Betsey	5
Judith	2	Netherland, Mrs. Elizabeth	
Kitty	14		65
Martha	78	Nevis, Betsey	5
Milly	88	Nicholson, Mary	64
Mitchell, Betsy	66	Norrill, Jane	86
Catharine	92	Norvell, Anna	46
Elizabeth	99	Martha	6
Milly	3	Salley	56
Nancy	38	Nowel, Jane	86

Nowell, Rebekah 95
Nowlin, Milley 14
 Polly 59
Nuchols, Mary 75
Nuckols, Betsey 106
 Betsy 17
 Elizabeth 68, 106
 Frances 87
 Jane 27
 Martha 68
 Martha M. 68
 Nancy 68
 Polly 21
 Polly Wooddy 87
 Susanna 96

O

Osborne, Judith 43
Owen, Kitty 79
 Polly 20

P

Pace, Anner 70
 Catharine 69
 Cyty 69
 Frances 83
 Jane 12
 Lucy 69
 Mary 47
 Rachael 46
 Susanna 43
Page, Betsey 88
 Betsy 106
 Caty 36
 Christian 86
 Elizabeth 64
 Frances 98
 Jane 97
 Janey 70
 Mary 36, 86
 Mary Ann 59
 Nancy 13, 44, 70
 Patsey 40
 Phany 17
 Susanna 40, 107
Parish, Polly M. 20
 Susannah 97
Parrish, Anna 86
 Betsy 34, 109
 Catharine 26
 Catherine 26

Parrish, Charity 52
 Constance M. 72
 Cynthia F. 74
 Dolly 71
 Elizabeth 8, 42
  (2) 71, 84
 Huldah B. 5
 Jane 57
 Judith 67
 Lucy 28
 Margaret 85
 Martha Holland 17
 Mildred 26, 72
 Permilia 71
 Polly 5, 103
 Rocksey 72
 Sally 60
 Sarah 50
 Susan A. 23
 Tabitha 1
Patterson, Betsey 79
Payne, Agathy 93
 Agnes 62
 Alice B. 32
 Ann O. 92
 Anna 15, 37
 Anne 33
 Catharine 7
 Dorothea D. 8
 Elizabeth 110
 Elizabeth F. 41
 Elizabeth McC. 74
 Frances 82
 Jane 8, 53
 Judith B. 53
 Margaret B. 74
 Martha 95
 Mary 89
 Nancy 29
 Sarah 93
 Susanna 38
 Susanna W. 35
Peers, Dorothea 109
 Dorothy 109
 Frances 75
 Judith 48, 88
 Nancy 60
Pemberton, Ann Coleman 20
 Cynthia 10
 Dice King 81
 Mary B. 11
Perkins, Ann 24, 39
 Ann R. 39

Perkins, Elizabeth   24, 54
      Elvira   75
      Judith   67
      Lucy A.   108
      Mary   29
      Mary G.   95
      Nancy   31
      Patsy   7
      Sarah   50
      Susanna   47
Pierce, Lucy   65
      Lydia`   19
      Susan   45
Pleasants, Ann Scott   105
      Anna R.   101
      Caroline R.   22
      Damaris   77
      Eliza P.   76
      Mrs. Elizabeth   111
      Elizabeth W.   9
      Eudosia   81
      Jane   76
      June   7
      Mariana L.   92
      Martha   95, 104
      Susanna Randolph   95
Pledge, Elizabeth- 77, 110
      Frankey M.   111
      Martha   17
      Mildred   106
      Nancy   32
      Ursula   82
Pollard, Elizabeth   62
      Jane   22
      Milly   74
Pollock, Polley   77
Poor, Elizabeth -6, 35, 41
      Jenny   32
      Judith   75
      Keziah   42
      Lucy   63
      Martha   78
      Martha S.   49
      Mary   78
      Mary G.   45
      Mildred   19
      Polly   45
      Sarah   10
      Susanna   30, 89
Pope, Nancy   101
      Polly W.   48
Potter, Mary   54
Povall, Elizabeth   87

Powell, Ann   67
      Elizabeth   33
      Polly   26
Powers, Elizabeth   71
      Judy Madison   44
      Mary Ann   52
      Sally   63
      Sarah   63
Preyear, Sarah   64
Price, Elizabeth   85
      Judith   29
      Lucy M.   67
Profit, Judith   2
Profitt, Nancy   2
Pryor, Judith N.   25
      Martha   62
      Mary   100
      Nancy   109
      Peggy   16
      Sally   74
      Sarah   74
Pulliam, Elizabeth   15
      Frances Mitchel   3
      Nancy Harris   22
      Sally R.   102
Puryear, Elizabeth   53, 111
      Jane   9
      Martha   92
      Mary Heth   42
      Milly Winn   66
      Nancy W.   68
      Patsy   67
      Polley   38
      Susanna   66
      Susanna Smith   60

Q

Quigg, Martha   82
      Mary A. S.   76
      Mary Ann S.   76

R

Radford, Elizabeth   104
      Sally Downs   21
Ragland, Ann   54
      Martha O.   63
      Polly M.   14
      Sarah   76
      Susan D.   91
Randolph, Anna   88
      Dorothea   109

Randolph, Elizabeth 77
    Gabriella 10
    Jane 46
    Judith 23, 94
    Mary 37, 54, 81
    Susanna 37
Reatherford, Eliza S. 9
Redd, Eliza R. 33
    Lucy W. 107
    Mary 60, 61
    Polly 23
    Sally 24
Reddy, Betsy 36
    Elizabeth 36
    Polly 68
    Sally 94
Redford, Ann Lewis 63
    Lucy 82
    Martha 32
    Mary 9, 27
    Mildred 110
    Nancy 109
    Patsey 32
Richards, Nancey 35
    Polly R. 72
    Sally 13
Richardson, Agnes 89
    Betsy J. 103
    Hannah 105
    Margaret 62
    Nancy 19
    Peggy 62
    Polly 85, 87
    Sally 24
    Sally M. 73
    Susanna 65
Ricks, Nancy 47
    Susanna 108
Riddle, ------ 108
    Anna 104
    Elizabeth 25
    Jenny 47
    Martha 32
    Mary 79, 108
Rigsby, Susanna 97
Robards, Sarah 50
Rogers, Jane 7
Roundtree, Sarah 24
Rountree, ----- 66
    Anna 48
Rowen, Nancy 57
Rowntree, Betty 3
    Elizabeth 22

Rowntree, Jane 11
    Martha 27
    Mary 33
Royster, Elizabeth 86
    Mary 7
    Prudence 101
    Susan H. 110
Rutherford, Eliza S. 9
    Elizabeth 26
    Mary 23
    Ursula 84
Ryan, Jane 1
    Morning 103
    Mourning 103
    Nancy 40

S

Sadler, Betsy 42
    Elizabeth 42
    Mourning 6
    Rosamond 96
    Sarah 10
Salmon, Elizabeth 46
    Jane 70
    Molley 13
Salmons, Elizabeth 46
    Jane 70, 87
    Mary 30
    Polly 70
Sampson, Elizabeth A. 85
    Jane 73
    Judith 78
    Martha 93
    Molly 78
    Nancy 25, 37
    Patsey 73
    Polly 75
Sanders, Betsy 34
    Jane W. 44
    Mary 14
    Nancy 4
    Susanna 104
Sandis, Mary 14
Satterwhite, Clara 13
    Frankey 106
Saunders, Betsy 3
    Jane W. 44
    Mary Ann 90
    Sally 110
    Susann 104
Scott, Barbara 91
    Elizabeth 35

Scott, Fanny 55
 Frankey 61
 Lucy 88
 Nancy 13, 67
 Patsy 30
 Peggy 93
 Polly 25
 Sally 100
Scrugs, Mary 43
Sharp, Sally 38
Shelton, Ann 36
 Elizabeth 35, 108
 Frances 40
 Marinda 3
 Massy 90
 Merenda 3
 Nancy 36
 Polly 89
Shepard, Betsy 56
 Martha 18
Shepherd, Elizabeth 82
 Frances 91
 Hannah 103
Sheppard, Susanna 79
Shields, Martha 102
Ship, Mary 8
Shoemaker, Nancy 98
Sims, Elizabeth 70
Sinklur, Sally 85
Skelton, Elizabeth 105
Sladyen, Mary 33
 Molly 79
Slayden, Betsy 38
 Mary 33
 Molly 79
Slaydyn, Martha 103
Slaydyon, Jenny 21
Smith, ----- 30
 Anna Maria 76
 Betsey 58
 Elizabeth 6, 37
 Judith 98
 Lucy 37
 Mary 64, 101
 Nancy 93, 111
 Sally 24, 80
 Susanna 107
Smyth, Lucy 37
Stanford, Mary 96
Stegar, Mary Netherland 95
Stovall, Tabitha 106
Stratton, Ann 93
Strong, Betsy 53

Strong, Mary 55
 Rachel 56
Swift, Elizabeth 15
 Mary 32
 Sarah 45

T

Talley, America A. 43
Tate, Elizabeth 91
 Salley 51
Tayler, Ursly 79
Taylor, Mary 104
 Peggy Rollins 13
Terry, Polly 52
Thomas, Ann 84
 Anne 33
 Betsy 105
 Elizabeth A. 71
 Levinia 83
 Mary 40
 Milly 35
 Nancy 8
 Sarah 64
Thomason, Patsey 71
Thomasson, Betsy 105
 Sally 72
Thompson, Sarah 95
 Susanna 46
Thurston, Betsy 25, 33
 Jonah 6
 Mary 12, 98
 Peggy 34
 Susanna 45
Tibbs, Mary 95
Tiller, Lucy 35
Tinkler, Sally 85
Tinsley, Eliza P. 85
Toler, Elizabeth 60, 66
 Elizabeth J. 68
 Mildred 6
 Milly 6
 Nancy 42, 99
 Salley 49
 Sarah J. 97
Tollor, Agnes 16
Tuggle, Frances 69
 Jane 53
 Patsey 79
Turner, Anney 23
 Elizabeth 15
 Frances 5
 Inphana 103

Turner, Lucy 65
    Mrs. Lucy 65
    Mary 99
    Molly 99
    Sarah 104
    Triphania 103
Turpin, Elizabeth 25

U

Underwood, Ann 25
    Elizabeth M. 22
    Mary 22
    Sarah 55
Utley, Catharine 53
    Elizabeth 101
    Ellener 108
    Jane 106
    Martha 7
    Sally 54
    Sarah 98
    Susa 106
    Susanna 89, 106

V

Vaughan, Ann (2)-5
    Arpasia 51
    Elizabeth Shields 74
    Kitty 50
    Martha M. 83
    Patty

W

Wade, Anna 45
    Elizabeth 50
    Jane 27
    Lucy 59, 107
    Mary 91
    Sally 98
Wadlow, Judith 93
    Susanna 51
Waldrop, Polly 51
Walker, Elizabeth 108
    Frances 20
    Milly 47
    Patsey 72
    Polley 98
    Rebecca 77
Walmack, Judith 23
    Nancy 23
Ware, Elizabeth 77

Ware, Jenny 65
    Judith 50
    Nancy 30, 111
Watkins, Eadith 83
    Elvira 108
    Jane 21
    Jane, Jun[r]. 60
    Judith 104
    Martha 20
    Martha T. 26
    Mary 49, 99
    Mildred 67
    Nancy 90
    Patsy 47
    Sarah L. 93
Webb, Ann 57
    Nancy 29
Webber, Betsy 30
    Ketturah 11
    Molly Linsy 81
    Polley 48
    Polly 49
    Salley 106
    Susanna 29
Webster, Elizabeth 69
White, Elizabeth 16
Whitlock, Catharine 106
    Sally 96
Whitt, Susanna 14
Williams, Mrs. Betsey 24
    Christian 34, 103
    Elizabeth 14, 71, 86, 106
    Fanny 69
    Frances 35
    Frances T. 18
    Lucy 1
    Sarah 21, (2)-54
Willis, Elizabeth 68
    Jane 101
    Lucey 16
    Mary 82
    Nancy 23
    Susanna 102
Wilmerton, Elizabeth 14
Windle, Sally 72
Winfield, Susanna 105
Wingfield, Elizabeth 84
    Frances 51
    Nancy 87
    Phebe 50
    Sally 4
    Sarah 4

Winston, Mary   25
Witt, Ann   67
    Elizabeth   59, 70
    Polly   107
Witte, Susannah   19
Womack, Mary   108
Wood, Elizabeth   18
    Liddia   34
    Lucy   103
    Mary   49
    Patty   62
    Sarah   80
Woodson, Agnes   100
    Ann   42
    Anna   109
    Elizabeth 45, 48, 50
          84, 86, 99, 110
    Fanny   28
    Jane   32, 54, 76
    Janey   17
    Judith   82
    Judith P.   77
    Maria V.   13
    Martha   81
    Mary   64, 65, 82
    Mary G.   3
    Nancey   77
    Paulina   110
    Polly   24, 109
    Salley   110
    Sally   29, 82
    Sally P.   55
    Sarah   27
    Susanna   17, 81, 82
    Susanna E.   10
    Tabitha   11
    Ursula   56
Woodward, Jane   11
    Lucey   106
    Lucy   106
    Rebecca   102
    Susannah   56
Woolbanks, Elizabeth   9
    Polley   7
Word, Celey   107
    Sealey   107
Wyatt, Lavinia C.   91

              Y

Young, Martha   75
Younger, Elizabeth   31
    Martha   75

INDEX TO SURETIES AND OTHERS

Adams, James 1, 32, 70, 84
  Thomas 73
  William 39
Addams, George 91
  James 84
  John 84
Addkinson, Isaiah 79
  Stephen 79
Allen, George 1
  James 33
  James, Jr. 41
  William 1, 12, 30, 80, 88
Allin, William 12
Alves, Shederick 12
Alvis, Charles 105
  David 2, 12, 16
  Elijah 12
  George 70, 71
  John 19, 86
  Judith 2
  Shadrack 2
  Zach. 102
  Zachariah 86, 104, 107
Alvys, Robert 93
Amos, Charles 83
  Francis 2
  Frans 24
Anderson, Benjamin 6, 17, 31, 47, 70, 73, 79, 101
  John 99
  Joseph 3, 109
  Katy 31
  Lawrence 7, 52, 97
  Matthew 42
  Meredith 4
  Meridith 45
  Richard 2, 25, 31, 90, 96
  Thomas M. 109
Archer, William 10
Armistead, Henry 33
Ashton, Daniel 67
Aston, Daniel 67, 87
  Samuel 36
Atkins, Judah 29
Atkison, Sarah 10

Atkins, Wm. 71
Atkisson, Joseph 97
Attikisson, Peter 58
Attkins, Henry 56
Attkinson, Josiah 44, 79, 107
Attkison, Judith 34
  Peter 3
  Thomas 44
  William 16, 56, 72, 79, 93
Attkisson, Charles 13, 25, 40, 59, 63, 76
  Henry 13
  Isaiah 27
  John 3
  Jonah 15
  Joseph 57, 61
  Judah 28, 73
  Pleasant 79
  Pleasant, Jr. 33
  Sally 37
  Thomas 107
Austin, Fleming 23, 58
  John 15, 23, 58
Ayers, Samuel 32

B

B_____, Thomas 7
Bailey, Callam 30
  Callom 54
  Callom H. 30
  Holman 92
  John G. 30
  Peyton H. 71
Baker, Clevears 4
  John 100
Baley, Thomas 31
Ball, James 4
Balleu, Leonard 50
Banks, Jacob 18, 19, 28, 98
  John 1, 19, 23, 56
Barett, Jane 23
  John 23
Barlow, Robert T. 97
Barner, Joshua 109
Barnett, Athanasius 88

Barnett, Elisha   28, 68
                             78
     George   24
     Hannah F.   78
     James   31
     Jean   4, 5
     John   4, 5, 32, 49
              68, 93
     Robert   49
     William   49, 68, 93
Barnit, John   88
Bartlett, Mary   68
Bass, John   74
Bassett, Thomas   14
Bates, Caroline W.   46
     Charles   99
     Charles F.   31, 56
                     94, 103
     Fred   71, 85
     Frederick   17, 87
     Isaac   17
     James   26
     Richard   1, 2, 25
          40, 41, 43, 44, 69
          72, 73, 86, 106
     T.   60
     Tar: 78, 80
     Tarleton   31
     Tarlton 31, 40, 103
     Thomas F. 12, 17, 103
     Thomas T. 31, 65, 86
Baugh, A. B.   13
     Burwell   40
Baughan, James   92
Bedford, Stephen   65
Bellamy, Bradley   5, 72
     Richard   6
     William   5
Bernard, Faney   67
     John   28, 55
     Joshua   28
Bevans, John   52, 103
Bibb, James   66, 102
     John   16, 28
     John, Jr.   16, 28
     Sarah   102
     William   16, 28
Bickley, Francis   12
Bigger, John   16
Binford, James   35
     Thomas   17
Binns, John   24

Blackburn, Roland   6
Blackwell, Jesse   11, 98
Blalock, Elebeth   91
     Elizabeth   26
     Hezekiah   26
     Jeremiah   91
Blanks, Robert   95
Blunkall, Robert   68
     William   21, 57, 110
Boatwright, John R.   49
     Richard   20
Bolling, John   54
     John, Jr.   54
     Robert   29
     Thomas   54
Borne, Stephen   80
Bourn, Lewis   35
Bourne, George   8
Bowles, Anderson   7
     Bartlet   97
     Bartlett   11
     Benjamin   9
     Deborah   9
     Elizabeth   9
     George   69
     Gideon   58, 67
     John   9, 76
     John, Jr.   9
     Sarah   58
     Thomas   8, 45
     W. K.   45
Bowman, Joseph   9
     Ned   88
Boyce, Daniel   92
Boyer, Sally   37
Bradshaw, Benjamin   31, 66
                           109
     Claburn   17
     Hannah   9
     John   9, 59
     John, Jr.   43
     Larner   103
     Learner   52
     Sarah   9
Bragg, John L.   97
Branch, Samuel   5, 9, 46
              82, 88, 96, 99
     Thomas   58
Britt, Bolling   21, 49
     Hannah   78
     John   39, 42, 49
     Martha   39

Britt, William 10, 39, 63
  William, Sr. 21, 78
Broaddus, Eliza S. 10
Brooks, Mayry 94
  Michel 94
  Peter 94
  Thomas 73, 89
  Walker 73, 89
Brown, Daniel 50
  John 11, 30, 36, 86
  Reubin I. 11
  Samuel 82
  W. 10
Browning, James E. 20
Brumfield, Elijah 101
  John 79
Bryce, Arch. 74
  Arch^d. 30, 73
  Archibald 55
  John 73, 74
Bryer, John 85
Bryers, John 49
Bullington, John 82
Bumpass, Garland L. 102
Bunch, Littleberry 106
Burch, Littleberry 106
  Margaret 48
  Reuben 11
  Reubin 11
Burford, Nathaniel 57
Burgess, William 57, 86
Burnley, Harden, Jr. 63
  John 80
Burruss, Nathaniel 63
Burton, Robert 12, 74
  Walthall 79
  William 12
Busby, James 12, 80
  William 12
Bush, John 111
  William 56
Butler, George 12

          C

Cabell, William 12
  William, Jr. 12
Caldwell, Thomas 38
Callis, Lavinia 94
Campbell, A. 100
  Francis L. 31
Cannon, John 9, 110
Carden, Jesse 13

Carden, Robert 27, 44
Cardin, David M. 91
  Robert 63
  Wilson 51
Carel, Buckear 6
Carr, G. 89
  Samuel 96
Carrell, Booker 36, 100
  David 7, 97
  Josiah 55
  Roger 13
  William 13
Carroll, Booker 95
Carter, James 30, 57
  Judith 86
  Mary 47
  Robert 108
  Susanna 97
  Thomas 47
  William 9, 35, 106
Carven, William 5
Cawthorn, Charles 9, 15
  James 9
Cawthon, Robert 93
Chancellor, David 19
  Julius 102
  Sarah 19
  Thomas 14, 19
Chaudoin, Lewis 41
Cheadle, John 76, 81
Cheatum, John 34, 40
Chick, Ambler 76
  William 50, 76
Childres, Nancy 51
Childress, Elijah 7
  John 94
  John G. 56, 75
  John J. 15
  John, Jr. 94
  Maden 94
  Nelson 34
  Patrick 94
  Richard 68
  Spotswood 15, 34, 48
            68
  William 15, 68
Chisholm, Cornelius D. 95
  David 15
  Hen. 33
  Nimrod 29
  Suprey 33
  Thomas 20, 102
  Walter, Sr. 33

Chisholme, Polly   90
Chitham, John   14
Chittum, Zacha R.   14
Chowning, George   78
Christian, Andrew   14
    Anthony   86
    Charles   15, 25, 109
    George   109
    Jacob   14
Clark, Christopher   26
    Elizabeth   31
    Macajah   26
Clarke, Daniel   84, 107
    Elisha   16
    Ellison   9
    Isham   16, 108
    Jeffry   1
    John   77, 91, 99
    Mary   41
    Peter   9
    Pleasant   34
    Stephen   1, 73
    Turner, Jr.   20, 37
          49, 54, 68, 77
    William   14, 92
Clarkson, Anselum   72
    David   17
    Jesse   31
    William   106
Clement, John   2
Clements, James,2, 43, 106
    James, Jr.   43
    Jesse   33, 43, 51
    John   7, 69
    Mary   47
    Sally   1
    Stephen   1, 47
Cliborne, William, Jr.   78
Clopton, Benjamin   44, 76
    Benjamin M.   76
    Mary   76
    Walter   36, 89, 103
Clough, George   17
    George, Jr.   17
Clyborne, William, Sr.   78
Cocke, Anne   61
    Benjamin   39
    Benjamin, Jr.   27, 43
          54, 68, 87, 109
    Benjamin, Sr.   17
    David P.   32, 74
    Jack F.   8

Cocke, James   8, 32, 40
         80, 84, 99, 110
    Jin   99
    Mary   40
    Nancy, Junr   61
    Pleasant   39, 47, 50
    Richard   33, 91
    Samuel   16
    Thomas   17, 54, 79
    William   15, 17, 76
                      81, 84
Cockran, Henry   18, 42
    James   18
    Jo   57
Cockrane, Mary   28
Cockrum, Henry   100
Cogil, John   24
Cole, James   4
Coleman, Robert   25, 54
                          62
Coles, Walter   90
    William D.   90
Coley, Pege   97
Colly, Charles   102
Colvard, William   46, 62
Coly, Elizabeth   97
Comer, Thomas   92
Coons, Richard   89
Cooper, Daniel   20
Copeland, Martin   32
Cosby, Meredith   38
    Samuel   100
Cousins, Francis   59
Cox, Bartlett   68
    Edward   86
    Edward, Jr.   58
    Henry   42, 97
    John   20
    Judith   97
    Trent   3
Crafton, Polly   25
Crank, Lipscomb   90
    Stephen   20, 89
Creely, Tarlton   104
Crenshaw, Asbury   81
    Benjamin   25, 91
    Benjamin, Jr.   89
    Benjamin, Senr   89
    David   52
    John   69
    Nathan   1
    Reuben   2, 3

Crenshaw, Thomas 25
Crouch, John 6, 27, 75
  Stephen 18, 21, 28
    34, 46, 50, 54, 55
    91, 98
  William 33
Crutchfield, John S. 15
  Nicholas 21
  Stapleton 4, 35
  Stephen 92
  William, Jr. 92
Curd, Edmund 21, 82, 104
  Isaac 26, 74
  James 69
  John 2, 22, 37, 63
    68, 79, 92, 99, 104
  Richard 82, 104
  Thomas 2, 37
Curle, John 33

D

Dabbs, Joseph 17, 33, 61
Dabney, Cornelius 94
  George 36
  Gwathmey 58
  Isaac W. 94
Dandridge, Archibald B. 25
    102
  Arch[d] B. 22, 29, 45
  John B. 25
  Mildred 22, 102
  N. W. 29
  Richard A. 65
  Robert 73
  Robert A. 22
  W. 45
  William 45, 81
Daniel, Ichabod 35
  John 22, 35
  Obadiah 22, 35
  Sally 35
Davenport, Benjamin 23,
    101
  John 107
  William 23
Davies, Nicholas 6, 94
Davis, John 31, 44
  John S. 23
  Larkin A. 23
  Shelton G. 31
  William 63

Deals, Jacob 97
Demue, Larose 19
Demure, Lawrous 25
Denton, John 48
  John, Jr. 48
  Suzanar 48
Deprest, Elizabeth 14
Dickenson, Henry H. 76
  John J. 17
  William 76
Dickerson, Thomas 58
Dickinson, John J. 3
Digges, John 96
  William 80, 81
Diggs, Dudley 80, 81
  Dudley, Jr. 100
  Dudley, Sr. 100
  William 80
  William, Jr. 81
Dimue, Larrose 69
  Larrows 19
Dismukes, Daniel 39
  Paul 19, 30, 61, 100
Douglass, Nich[s] 62
  Rev. William 62
Dowdy, Elizabeth 13, 53
  John 36
Drayke, Sary 69
Drumwright, George, 7, 61, 80
  Capt. George 57
  Thomas 80
  Washington 25, 52
  William 9, 10
Duke, Benjamin B. 59
  Cosby 24
  Edmund 24
  Fontain 25
  Fountain 100
  Sary 24
  Thomas 3
Dunn, John 89
Dunnavant, Thomas 25
Duval, Benjamin 100
  Claborne 36

E

Easly, Rodrick 26
East, Benjamin 13
Eastin, Augustine 101
Edwards, James 26
Elam, William 92

Eldridge, John B.   39
        Thomas   19, 39, 47
        Thomas, Jr.   64, 92
Ellis, Charles   27
        Daniel   108
        David   27
        Harris   27
        John   55
        John Smith   9
        Joseph   55
        Joseph S.   41
        Pattey   75
        Stephen   27, 41, 108
        Thomas   27
England, David   93
Eubank, Stephen   83
Evans, Archer   50, 98

                F

Fagg, William   16
Fargerson, Charles   40
Faris, Charles   5
        John   85
        Joseph   56
        Lemuel   107
        Sary   85
Farmer, John   33
        Thomas   27, 66
Farrar, Barrat   5, 83
        Barrett   28
        Elizabeth   5
        Frances   36
        John   28, 93, 109
        Joseph   28
        Ro.   30
        Robert   64, 105
        Thomas   5, 28
        Will   11
        William   14, 28, 29
                    30, 99, 111
        William, Jr.   29, 36
Faudree, Joseph,28, 29, 97
        Major   73
        Thomas   56
Finch, John   99
Fitzpatrick, Joseph   29
Fleming, John, Jr.   6
        Mary   65
        Tarlton   6, 105
        Thomas   74
Flournoy, John James   1
Ford, Elizabeth   27

Ford, John   38, 44
        Mary   30
        Reuben   30
        Reuben, Jr.   28, 30
        Thomas   26, 51, 65
        William   65
Foster, John   44
        William   85
Fowler, Alexander   11, 61
                        85, 94
        Alexander, Jr.   111
        Alexander, Sr.   30
        Jacob B.   17, 61, 94
        Sherwood   30
Fox, Judith   31
Fraser, Donald   34
French, Mason   43
        Mason, Jr.   83
        Robert   38, 43, 85
        Saley   43
Fretwell, John   39
        Morning   39
        Richard   39
Fulcher, John   31, 39, 61
Fuqua, William   25, 96
Furlong, John   96
        John, Sr.   34
Fuzmore, Edward,19, 56, 89
        Isaac   88

                G

Gammon, John   32, 87
Gardner, Thomas   83
Garnett, James   36
Garthwright, Absalom   77
Gay, Thomas B.   29
        William   29
Geirden, James   62
        Sarah   62
Gennatt, Thomas   25
George, James   18, 23, 32
            41, 73, 100, 101
        James, Sr.   32
        William   22, 32, 93
                              94
        William, Jr.   75
Gilbert, John   50
Gill, John   1, 16
Gilliam, John   17, 52, 71
                              74
        William   15
Gilmer, Pichey Ridgway   55

Gilpin, Alban 76
   Thomas 19
Glass, David 2, 7, 12, 32
                33, 104
   James 33, 52
   John, Jr. 90
   John, Sr. 90
   William 90
Glenn, Robert 19
Gooch, John 35
Goodloe, George 41
Goodmon, Charles 59
Gordin, Benjamin 55
   William 55
Gordon, James 53
   John 28, 55, 85
Grainge, Stephin 98
Grant, Alexander 92
   Alex^r 86
   John 34, 92
Graves, James 51, 68
   John 1
   Lucy 1
   Ralph 79
   Rice 26, 68, 77, 85
   Snead 1
Gray, Harry 14
   Henry 7, 15, 31, 72
             109, 111
   Henry, Jr. 37
   Henry, Sr. 37
   John 15
   Joseph 65, 103
   Susanna 56, 77, 89
   William 37, 101
   William H. 15
Green, Forrester, Jr. 99
   John 2, 12, 15, 28
   Thomas 14, 20
   William 27, 102
Gresham, Elizabeth 25
   James 15, 25, 26, 62
   James, Jr. 25
   Mary 15
   William 25
Groom, Henry M. 8
   William 2
Grooms, Robert 34
Grubb, Andrew 80
   Daniel 15, 31, 80
   Jesse 15
Grubbs, Daniel 96

Grubbs, John 2
   Matthew 87
Guerrant, D. 27, 37, 81
   John 34
   John, Jr. 69
Guinn, Edward 18

H

Haden, Anthony 107
   Jesse 35
   John N. 19
   Joseph 35
   Ro. 26
   Robert 78
   William 46
   Zachariah 9, 78
Hall, Jane 20, 67
   Jeney 62
   Janie 23
   William 35, 104
   William W. 67, 69
Halsey, James 13
Hamner, John 28
Hancock, George 3
   Major 64, 70, 91
   Major, Jr. 69, 70
   Tene 111
Hancocke, Major 2
Hardin, Elizabeth 32
   Thomas 32
Harding, Giles 64
   Thomas 44, 74, 100
               110
   William 12, 78
Hardwick, Christopher 84
Harris, Harrison 39
   James 29
   John 29, 86
   John, Jr. 47
   John L. 15, 32, 37
       48, 63, 89, 101
      103, 107, 108
   John Z. 86
   William 29, 36, 85
           110, 111
Harrison, Andrew 103
   William 37, 100
Harvie, John 57
   John, Jr. 57
Hatcher, Gideon 6, 37
   J. L. 37

Hatcher, Josiah, Jr.   36
    Sarah   21
    Thomas   21, 53
Hathorn, William   38
Hawthorn, Rebecca,104, 106
    William   106
Heale, George   38
    William   4
Helms, Sarah   24
    William   79
Henderson, Elizabeth   77
    Sarah G.   91
Henley, Hezekiah   37
    Patrick   67
    William   75
Herndon, Benjamin   39
    Isbel   95
    John   39, 89, 99
    Lewis   11, 39
    Susannah   95
Hicks, John   6, 91, 96
    Mary   39
    Meshack,6, 13, 39, 96
    Moses   39
    William   36
Higgason, Samuel   1, 39
Hines, Henry   72
    John   50, 98
    R. D.   36
    Tarlton   39
Hix, J.   17
    William   14, 28, 60,
                              91
Hodges, Frances   56
    James   6
    Jesse   8, 50, 70, 84
                              97
    Johnson   40, 70, 95
                              98
    Lewcy   70
    Robert   56
    Thomas,1, 54, 56, 102
    Thomas, Jr.   2
    Welcome William   50
                             104
    William   17, 27, 69
                         97, 104
        William, Jr.   45
        William, Sr.   40
Hodneth, John   94
Hogan, John   21, 94
Hoggatt, Anthony   22
Holbrook, Randall   73

Holeman, John   41
Holland, James   41
    John   1, 107
    George   12, 51, 53
    George, Sr.   41
    John   41, 44
    Michael   12, 41
    Michael, Sr.   41
    Nathaniel   17, 96
Holman, James   38
    George   3, 54
    Susannah   42
    William   30, 34, 38
                     39, 62, 107
    William M.   6
Hood, Thomas   63
Hooper, Daniel   4
    Joseph   61
Hope, Thomas A.   80, 96
                             100
Hopkins, Anderson   20
    Arthur   46, 61
    Benjamin   89
    Charles   82, 95
    Charles, Jr.   56, 77
    George W.   31
    Henry   31
    J.   31, 83
    James   21, 32, 49, 54
    John   12, 101
    Nelson   20, 106
    Rowland   31
Hopper, Milley   70
    Tabitha   68
Horner, Bartlett   18
Houchins, Francis   2
    Joice   2
    Joshua   10
Howe, Thomas   101
Howell, Aise (Isaac)   45
    Charles   4
    Iisac   88
    Judith   88
    Junior   45, 88
    Patsy   10
    William   4
Howle, Absalom   65
Huddleston, Margareat   62
    Robert   27
Hudson, David   8
    George   49
Hughes, Benjamin   14
    James   81

Hughes, John 33
    Robert 110
    William 33, 75, 87
                  101
      William, Jr. 75
Hughson, John 47, 48, 108
Humber, John 19, 76
    John, Jr. 46
    John, Sr. 58
Hume, Alexander 38
Hunnicutt, M. 57
Hunter, Allen 4
    Austin 94, 100
    Forris 47, 49
    Fountain D. 94
    George 37
    Lewis 109
Hutchins, Strangeman 74
Hutsin, John 65
Hyde, Ann 26
    Robert 26
Hylton, Judith S. 29

I

Isaacs, Austin 46
Isbell, Benjamin 89, 99
    Christopher 109
    Henry 41
    William 91, 93

J

Jackson, Elisha 8
    John 8, 39
    Thomas 17
James, John 41
    Martin 45, 52
    Thomas 39, 41, 52
    William 40, 53
Jarratt, Alexander 73
    Ann 7, 20
    Archelus 73
    David 7
    Deux 73
    Devereux 45, 64, 73
    Dev[x]. 73
    Robert 7, 36, 46, 49
    William 73
Jarrett, Deux 16
    Lucy D. 43
Jenkins, Anthony 46
Jennings, Samuel 65

Jennitt, Elizabeth 33
Johnson, Benjamin 38, 44
    47, 48, 58, 60, 69, 79
    90, 94, 103, 108
    Benjamin, Jr. 48
    Charles, 46, 48, 51, 95
    Charles, Sen[r] 5
    Clabourn 16
    Collin 42
    Daniel, 47, 49, 79, 104
    David 79, 92, 93, 97
    David, Jr. 47, 79
    Elizabeth 46, 95
    G. 31
    Isham 79
    Jacob 20, 54, 97
    James 54, 71, 79
               83, 93
    Jane 97
    Jed[n]. 31
    Jedidiah 8, 96
    John 46, 90, 104
    John W. 48
    Joseph 46
    Richard 37, 53, 103
    Robert 86
    Stephen 58, 84, 107
    William 17, 24, 42
         58, 78, 85, 93
         109, 110
Jones, Dabney H. 25
    David, Sr. 50
    John B. 42
    Landy 8
    William H. 50
Jordan, Charles 12
    Charles F. 98
    Charles, Sr. 50
    James 50
    John 50
    Matthew 50
    Samuel 50
Jorden, John 62
Jouett, John, Jr. 80

K

Kannon, Elizabeth 37
    William 37
Kearsey, George 72
Keeps(?), Mary 62
Kellshaw, John 71
Kennedy, James 104

Kerr, Charles   38, 45
Kersey, Alexander   36
    Alex^n   51
    Garland   72, 107
    Henry   91
Key, Joshua   51
    Martin   49
King, Higgason   51
    Peter   83

L

Lacy, Charles   72
    Elliot   34, 48
    Elliott   26
    Jesse   48
    Matthew   8, 32, 66
    Nancy   104
    Stephen   85
    Susanah   36
    Susanna   4, 104
Lain, Sherod   50
Lane, Anthony   62
    John   25
    Stephen   70
    William   67, 75
Lanior, David   23
Laprade, John   6, 32, 37
    63, 74, 93, 96, 108
    John, Jr.   74
    Susanna,6, 34, 74, 81
    Susannah   93
Lawrence, Elizabeth   52
    John   45, 52
Lawson, Philip   4, 16, 48
                       99
Layne, Anthony   21, 35, 61
    Aris   9
    Claborne   98
    David   14, 23, 52
                   90, 98
    Elisha   12
    Frederick   98
    George   10, 49, 53
                   67, 71
    Jacob   59
    Jesse   84
    John   16, 25, 49
                72, 96, 109
    Richard   30
    Tarlton   52, 96
    William   19
Leak, Josiah   109

Leake, Elisha   5, 47, 69
              78, 79, 103
    Josiah   1, 45, 69
    Walter   39, 45, 49
Lee, John   31, 69
Leforce, Rene   14
Leitch, James F.   30
Lemay, Samuel   46, 63
Leprade, John   77
Lewis, Charles   51, 55, 84
    Howell, Sr.   54
    John   3, 17, 35, 55
           58, 61, 65, 82
           84, 88, 91
    John, Jr.   51
    Joseph,65, 80, 82, 84
    Nicholas   50
    Richard   54
    Robert   54, 55
    Col. Robert   55
    Robert, Jr.   54
    Warner   54
    William   16, 18, 55
                   84, 89
Linch, James Head   2
Logan, Alexander   86
    Harriot   57
Loury, Matthew   98
    Matthew, Jr.   98
Lovell, Elizabeth   42
    George   8, 11, 73
                   76, 80
    William   56, 65
Low, John   92
Lowry, James   105
    Mathew, Jr.   57
    Mathew, Sr.   57
    Noel   34
Loyd, Thomas   3
Lynch, Polley   4
    Robert   4
    Thomas   28

Mc

McBride, Edward   61
    Elizabeth   9
    John   9
    Robert A.   7
McCard, Richard   39
McCaul, Stoakes   82
    Stokes   27, 36, 110
    William   36, 110

McDonald, Angus   64
McKeane, Willis   71
McKim, Alex^r   26
    Andrew   26
    Robert   26
McKoy, Daniel   102
McLaren, Daniel   40

M

Maddocks, James   22
Maddox, Clarkson   62
    David   27, 110
    James   49
    Jesse   99
    Josiah   106
    Mary   31
    Polly   110
    William   31
    Wilson   69
Madox, Mary   4
Mallory, Claiborne   29
    Sally   58
Mangam, Joseph   6
Mann, Mary   55
Mantlo, John   47
Marshall, Carter   24
    John   99
Martin, Anthony   41
    Edward   76
    Henry   60
    Jacob   19, 23, 42
    John   4, 50, 66
        94, 103
    Mitchel   49
    Ned   58
    Nelson   74
    Robert   59, 63, 108
    Samuel   45, 63, 88
        107, 108
    Suke   59
    Thomas   57, 59
    William   57, 59, 60
        83
Marye, James   88
Mason, Elizabeth   103
Massie, Benjamin   93
    Charles   33, 80
    David   53
    Fleming   11, 20
    Frances   60
    Gideon   43, 63
    Nathaniel   60, 62, 84

Massie, Thomas   76, 107
    Thomas, Jr.   80, 105
    William   32, 60, 104
    William, Jr.   104
Mastin, David   58
Mathews, Polley   23
Matthews, Edward, 18, 40, 48
        58, 60, 61, 78
    Edward, Jr.   18
    John   5, 6, 75, 109
    John W.   6, 23
    Nancy   109
    Sharod   43
    Thomas   5
    Thomas, Jr.   60
May, Charles   32
    Charles M.   6
Mayo, Edward   77
    George   99
    Robert   38
    Stephen   61, 93
Meanly, Dennett   41
    Elizabeth   41
    Francis   41
Menely, Richard   41
Meredith, James   24
    Pleasant   40
Meriwether, David   55
    Francis   55
    James   22
    Nicholas   37, 62
    Robert   25
    Thomas   41, 72
    William   37, 61, 62
        78, 80, 111
Michaux, Jacob   13
Michell, Arch^s   75
    William   73, 74
Michie, John   60, 81
Miller, Elizabeth   79
    Heath J.   34
    John   12, 32, 79
    Mary   81
    Sarah   83
    Thomas   38, 60, 81
    Thomas, Jr.   18
    W.   45, 51, 70
        82, 86, 88, 98
    W., Jr.   103
    William   7, 10, 11, 14
        15, 21, 22, 26, 29
        36, 41, 50, 51, 53
        56, 57, 60, 62, 67
        70, 77, 79, 81, 88
    89, 102, 103, 107, 111

Miller, William, Gent 83
    William H. 62, 83
    William, Jr. 41
Mills, William 45
Mimms, David 109
Mims, D. 63
    David 83
    David, the elder 2
    David, Jr. 2
    Drury 83
    Duguid 15
    Elizabeth 40
    Gideon,14, 17, 76, 78
    Jane 40
    Lisbeth 78
    Martha 63
    Martha A. 43
    Martin 47
    Robert 40, 43, 47
       78, 88, 90, 95
Mitchel, Benjamin 76
Mitchell, Anne 66
    Archelaus 63
    David 23
    John 23
    John D. 23
    Thomas 99
    William 83
Moody, John M. 4
    Mary A. 67
Moore, Amos Ld 28, 59
    Ann C. 81
    John 59
    John S. 22
Moreland, Wright 39
Morgan, Robert 51
Morris, Edward 67
    Nathaniel G. 110
    Robert 51
Morrison, John 50
Morrissette, Margaret 14
Morton, Ann 26
Mosby, Benjamin 62, 65
    Kezia 85
    Robert, Jr. 75
    William 85
Moseley, William 65
Mosley, James 97
    Joseph 97
    Kerz. 22
Moss, Alexander 24
    Benjamin 18
    Dover 80

Moss, Forest 80
    Hugh 26
    John, Jr. 57
    Richard 65
    Samuel 7, 66, 80
    Samuel D. 80
    Susanow 7
    William 2, 7
Mossley, William 63
Mullins, Conaley 10
    Conerley 8
    Daniel 106
    David 100
    Jesse 27, 106
    John 10, 106
    William 8, 57
Mullis, Anne 36
Mundin, John P. 87
Murray, David 9, 23
Murrell, Drury 28
Murrer, Benjamin 66
    Philip 106
Murry, Isaac 56
Muse, William 43
Myers, Joseph 53

N

Napier, Booth 9
    Bouth 75
Nelson, Thomas 10
Netherland, John 65
    Wade 65
Nevis, John 5
Nicholls, Thomas 41
Nichols, Harris 64, 88
Nightingale, Matthew 14
Noell, Samuel 95, 106
Norvell, James 46
    John 50
    Thomas 6, 56
Nowell, Samuel 13
    Thomas 86
Nowlin, Abraham 14
    Ann 59
    Stephen 59, 86
    Stephen, Jr. 52
Nowling, Elizabeth 39
Nuchols, Nancy 75
    Thomas 75
Nuckles, Charles 21
Nuckols, Andrew 38
    Benjamin 68, 87

Nuckols, Charles 68
  John 68
  Nelson 68
  Overton 68
  Pouncey 68, 96
  Pouncy 68
  Samuel 21
  William 17, 68, 87
  William A. 68

O

Oglesby, Richard 82
Opie, George H. 38, 78
Overstreet, Frances 100
Owen, David A. 20
  Kitty 87
  William 20

P

Pace, Edward 47
  Frances 69, 83
  Francis 46
  Jeremiah 90
  Jesse 69
  Joseph 43, 69
  Murray 47
  Murry 83
  Robert 47
  Stephen 83
Page, Dabney 59
  James, 36, 40, 64, 106
  Jesse 70
  John 40, 70, 88, 106
  Leonard 70
  Lewis 36, 69
  Mary 36, 64
  Matthew 77
  Reuben 44
  William 13, 40, 70
    86, 97, 106, 107
  William, Jr. 17, 97
  William, Sr. 17
Parish, Booker 20, 97
Parrish, Aaron 28, 50, 52
  Abram 59
  Alexander 71
  Allen 8
  Ann 71
  Anne 71
  Booker 5, 72, 85, 86
  Charles 71

Parrish, Corbin 71
  Dabney 10, 60, 71
  David 17, 85, 86
  David M. 23, 32, 72
    94
  Elizabeth 52
  George 60
  George W. 20, 51
  Humphrey 60
  James 5
  Joel 8
  John 1, 71, 72, 91
  John C. 72
  John Fleming 6
  John T. 5
  Jolly 52
  Mager 72
  Major 84
  Meredith 71
  Micajah 10, 24, 34
    71, 72
  Moses 1
  Robert 5, 103
  Sary 52
  Sherd 26, 49, 96
  Sherrard 42
  Sherwood, 23, 59, 71, 72
  William 26, 67, 71
    72, 86
Parsons, Augustus 72
  Margaret S. 77
  Samuel 72
  Woodson 72
Patterson, John 101
Payne, Agatha 35
  Alexander S. 11
  Ann 62
  Arch. 8, 38, 91
  Archer 4, 8, 95
  Archer, Jr. 8, 29, 95
  Archibald 7
  Archibald, Jr. 7
  Cuffy 45
  Fleming 1, 28, 40, 41
    50, 60, 75, 91
  G. 69, 78, 79, 80
    86, 90, 96
  George, 3, 5, 9, 12, 24
    27, 32, 40, 41, 62
    63, 75, 77, 81, 84
    85, 89, 91, 105,
    107, 111
  George, Jr., 15, 32, 38

Payne, George, Sr.   110
    George Woodson 11, 55
    Jesse   30, 74, 75
               82, 99
    John   4, 38
    Col. John   33
    John C.   49
    John, the elder 53
    Johnne   41
    John R. D.   73
    John W.   40
    Jos.   11
    Joseph   93
    Joseph M.   101
    Josias 37, 62, 73, 74
    Josias, the elder 38
    Josias, Jun[r]   73, 77
              99, 105
    Josias, Sr.   74
    Judith   12
    Margaret   77
    Richard   53, 73
    R. B.   29
    Robert   77
    Robert, Jr.   37
    Roderick P.   77
    Rod. P.   111
    Sally   35
    Tarleton   41, 92
    Tarlton   22, 32, 44
    Tarlton F.   92
    Thomas 6, 22, 23, 94
    William   37
Peatross, R. W.   111
Peers, Anderson   6, 88
            94, 109
    Andrew   94
    E.   75
    Thomas   79
Pemberton, Thomas 11, 20,
                81
Pendleton, William G. 93
Perkins, Arch.   83
    Arch[d]   39
    Archelaus   31
    Arch[s]   50, 75, 95
    Constant   24, 29
    Ezekiel   75
    George   33, 107
    Grief   50, 76
    Isaac O.   95
    John   44
    Joseph   24, 54

Perkins, Joseph, Jr.   2
    Judah   29
    Mary   29
    Nathaniel   75
    Robert   2, 3, 25, 90
               96
    Stephen   68
    Walker   75
    William   10, 63, 77
             108
    William, Jr.   108
Phaup, Benjamin   13, 19
             102
Phillips, George   42
Philpotts, John, Jr.   30
          55, 82
Pierce, John   19
    Milly   19
    William   82
Pleasants, Arch[d] 64, 76
             110
    Cary   95
    Isaac   15
    Isaac W.   95, 111
    James   95, 105
    James, Jr.   92
    James M.   77
    John G.   77
    Joseph   81
    J. W.   101
    Lucius C.   77
    Lucy W.   95
    Matthew   81
    Philip   9
    Reuben   81
    Reubin   59
    Richard   91, 104
    Robert   79, 91
    Robert Cary   105
    Sally   76
    William   95
Pledge, Ann   32
    Arch.   32
    Archer   77, 82, 100
    Francis   64
    John W.   32
    Martha   77
    William   17, 60, 77
             111
    William, Jr.   77
Poindexter, William,38, 51
             107
Pollard, Joseph   62, 74

Pollard, Joseph, Jr.	22	
Joseph, Sr.	22	
Pollock, John	37, 43, 67	
	77, 85, 90	
Thomas	78	
Thomas W.	60	
Ponton, William	99	
Poor, Abraham	19, 63	
Ann	35	
James	45, 63, 78	
Janey	19	
John	75	
Lucy	32	
Milley	35	
Robert	42, 52, 78	
Thomas	10, 19, 32	
	35, 45, 49	
	75, 78, 89	
William	25, 75	
Pope, Thomas	48, 58, 66	
	101	
Porter, Daniel	105	
Powell, William,	33, 67, 109	
William, Jr.	7	
William, Senr	26	
Power, Madison	67	
Powers, James	52	
John W.	44, 89	
Madison	71, 83	
Major	63	
Robert	28, 97, 99	
William	63, 71	
Price, Bourn	38	
Joseph	85, 93	
Leonard	29	
Merth	108	
Samuel	79	
William	54	
Profit, Samuel	107	
Proffitt, Samuel	83	
Profitt, Jesse	2	
George	49	
Sary	2	
William	80	
Pruitt, Abra	80	
Harrod	25, 80	
Pryer, Thomas	85	
Pryor, John W.	16	
S.	16	
Sally	93	
Samuel	26, 74, 93	
Will	12, 80	
William	25, 55, 62	
	74, 82, 92, 103	

Pryor, William, Sr.,	100, 109
Pulliam, John A.	81
Nelson, C.	81
Robert	81
Robert J.	22, 91
Thomas W.	22
Thompson W.	22, 102
William	22, 29, 102
Zachariah	3, 15
Puryear, Ann,	9, 38, 67, 111
Ellis	30
Hezekiah	38, 66, 83
	108
Hezh	81
Joseph	100
Obadiah	92
Thomas	44
Thomas H.	9
William	38, 67

Q

Quarles, John	53
Thomas	83
Quigg, James	18, 53, 82

R

Ragland, Dudley	54, 63, 75
Finch	23, 91
James	63
Joel	101
Randolph, A.	10
Archd	37
Brett	81
Isham	37
Thomas	37
Thomas M.	77, 81
Thomas Mann	105
William	94
Read, Jesse	32
John K.	53
Redd, Jesse	23, 77
John	81
Lucy W.	24
Mary	24, 33, 107
Molley	23
Sally	33
Reddy, William	36, 94
Redford, Edward	27, 82
Frances W.	23
Frank W.	110
Pearin	48
Richard	24, 27, 82

Redford, William   9, 82
                           110
Rice, Charles   99
    Philip A.   23
Rich, Jeremiah   17
Richards, John   72, 87
    William   13, 35
Richardson, David   51
    George   24, 62, 63
                      87, 103
    John   8
    Robert   65
    Samuel   85
    William   73
    William M.   75
Ricks, Gilbert   47, 108
    Nicholas   47
Riddle, Archer   25
    Archibald   25
    John   1, 101, 104
    Joseph W.   47
    Mathew   108
    Thomas   32, 47, 74
                          104
Rigsbey, Susannah   84
Rigsby, David   97
    Susanna   97
    William   84
Robards, G.   80
    James   83
    John   84
    Lewis   50
    Sarah   84
    Susannah   63
    William   65, 77, 83
                           84
Robertson, Andrew   4
    Robert J.   102
Robinson, George   38
    James   104
    Michael   4
Roundtree, Randol   24
    Sarah   51
Rountree, William   66
Rowntree, Randal   22, 33
    Randall   85
    Samuel   11, 27, 85
    Thomas   27, 92
    William   3
Royster, David   86
    John   92
    John H.   12, 85
    Joseph A.   12

Royster, Mary   110
    Thomas   34, 41, 85, 86
Rutherford, Archibald   71
    John   40, 48, 84
    Molly   84
    Samuel   9
    Will.   9
    William   17, 22, 23
                   26, 66, 84
Ryan, James   37, 86
    Joel   64
    Whitehead   1, 86
    William   38, 40

                S

Sadler, Benjamin 6, 9, 96
    Benjamin, Jr.   10
    Jesse   96
    Nancey   42
    William   42
Salmon, Benjamin   13
    James   70
    John   46
Salmons, John   70
    William, Jr.   87
Sammons, James   58
Sampson, Capt.   66
    Jane   100
    Richard   37, 85
    Stephen,10,60, 78, 93
    Stephen, Jr.   13, 73
    William   31, 66, 78
Sanders, David   70
    John   14
    Nelson, A.   44
    William   4, 34, 44
Sandidge, William   87
Satterwhite, James   87
    John   25
Saunders, David   70
    John   82
    Reuben   72
    Robert   90
    Robert H.   110
    Ro: H.   92
    Salley   104
    Turner A.   44
    William   42, 88
Scott, Elizabeth   55, 91
    Joseph   18, 67, 88
    Joshua   88
    Riley   30

Scott, William 61, 93
Scrugs, Richard 43
Seems, Nathan 75
Shapard, James 56
Sharp, Martin 38
Shaw, Middleton 23
Shelburne, William, Jr.108
Shelton, James 1, 8, 59
  James D. 32, 48, 90
  John 25, 30, 35
    36, 89, 108
    John, Jr. 90
    Joseph 74
    Peter 40
    Ro. 100
    Thomas 3, 37, 90, 95
Shepard, James, Sr. 18
  Robert 27, 87
Sheppard, Peter 90
Sherwin, Sam 35
Ship, William 7
Shoemaker, Thomas 56
  Thomas, Sr. 91
Shomaker, Thomas 49
Sims, John 91
Sinkclear, Arch^d 92
Sinklur, Micajah 85
Sizer, John 76
Skelton, Reuben 105
Sladgen, Major 57
Sladyen, William 79, 103
Slayden, Daniel 33
Slaydon, William D. 21
Smith, Edward 93
  G. 76
  George 24, 30
  George S. 12, 24, 37
    93
  J. 88
  James 92
  John 12, 26, 29
    53, 64, 99
  John, Jr. 72
  M. 9, 37, 81
  Marcellas 76
  Marcellus 104
  Mard. 15
  Mary 93
  P. 111
  Preston,20,33, 36, 42
    45, 64, 74, 88, 93
  Robert 80, 109
  Robert S. 69

Smith, Thomas 37
  Thomas Ballard 50
  William 103
  William S. 93
  William Sharp 31
Snead, Elizabeth 2
Soule, Rufus 57
Southall, Stephen 49
Southworth, George 59
  Stephen 29
  Thomas 93
Spears, John 46
Spurlock, William 111
Stamps, William 12
Stanley, Christopher 49
Starke, Thomas 62
Starkey, Elizabeth 51
  Joseph 51
Stevenson, George 50
Stone, William 36
Straugham, Bendall 103
Strong, Ann 55
  Nathan 53, 56
  Nathan, Jr. 56
  Thomas 56, 100
Swift, Charles 45
  Clevears 45
  Margarret 32
  Maria 15
  Sarah 32
  Thomas 15
  William 32
Sydnor, Ro. 17
Sym, Elisha 55

T

Tate, John 6
  Susanna 34
Taylor, John 13
  Robert 35
  William 35
  William T. 13
Terrell, Charles 13, 76
Terry, James 54
Thacker, Elisha 18
Thomas, Charles 84, 97
  James 8, 64
  Richard 8, 40, 43
Thomasson, George 105
  Hyllard 72
  Thomas 71, 72
Thompson, Nathaniel 17

Thompson, William L.   2
Thomson, David   39
Thornton, Francis   29
Thurman, John   50
Thurston, Elizabeth   6, 34
      George   98
      John   98
      John, Senr   98
      Meriwether   98
      William   4, 25, 45
      William, Jr.   98
      William R.   98
Tibbs, Sary   95
Tiler, Francis   98
Tiller, James   58
Tinsley, John   58
      Phillip   62
      Thomas   98
Todd, John   35
Toler, George   49, 60, 99
      Lemuel   47
      Mary   68, 97, 99
      Richard   42
Tollor, Susaner   16
Toney, John   31
Travilian, John   74
Trent, Edward   5
Trevilian, John   26
Triplett, Daniel   67
      John R.   67
Tuggle, Henry   53, 79, 100
      James   79, 99
Turnbull, Charles   107
Turner, Hardin   15
      Lewis   14, 15, 76
      Nancy   100
      Pleasant   23, 39, 105
      Reuben   18, 47, 74
      William   4, 5, 9, 23
                24, 34, 40, 65
                    99, 103
Turpin, Thomas   94
Tyler, George   18
      John   28

                U

Underwood, Alexander   101
      Edm^d   15
      Elizabeth   55
      Fr.   52, 94
      Francis   35, 53, 63
                74, 78, 94

Underwood, Francis, Jr. 22
      George   22, 100
      George, Jr.   22
      James   101
      John   57
Utley, David   101
      Hezekiah   53, 107
      Heziki   106
      John   101
      Obadiah   98
      Obediah   7, 53
      Reuben   89
      William 54, 106, 108

                V

Vaughan, James   90
      James, Jr.   51
      John   36
      Mary   51
      Matthew, 5, 38, 74, 88
      Nicholas   4
      Nicholas M.   15
      Shadrack   5
Vincent, William   107

                W

Wade, Ambrose   46, 102
      Austin M.   107
      Dabney   107
      Dabney, Jr.   102
      Daniel   46, 59, 102
      Daniel, Jr.   39
      Robert   24, 27, 50
                        98
      Thomas   91
      William   45
Wadlow, Thomas   51, 93
Waldrop, Francis   51
Walker, Agnes   6
      Anselm   11
      Austin   10, 45
      Hanselm   11
      Pete   9
      Peter   41, 77
      Shadrach   98
      Shadrack 20, 47, 72
      Thomas   62
      William   42, 53, 102
Walmack, Richard   23
Wamack, Richard   23
Ware, Andrew   55

Ware, James   30, 65, 103
    John   65, 77, 111
    John, Junr   65
    Mildred   65
    Nicholas   103
    William   100
Watkins, Ben   20
    Benjamin   26, 49, 83
    Benjamin P.   90
    George W.   22, 24
        33, 37, 42, 50
        85, 93, 103
    G. W.   98
    James   13, 100
    Jane   60
    Joseph   3, 60, 90
            100
    Joseph D.   26, 47
    Mary   104, 108
    Mayo C.   104
    Peter   26
    Susanna   60
    Thomas   60, 67
    Thomas B.   104
Weatherspon, Reubin   23
Webb, George   29
    George, Sr.   105
Webber, John   30
    Joseph   81
    Phil.   54
    Philip   11
    Sally   30
    William   30, 49, 81
            106
Weber, Philip   29
Webster, John   87, 105
    William   87, 107
West, George   12
    Mary   105
    Robert   105
White, John   8
    Lucy   8
Whitlock, Ann   105
    James   88
    Turner R.   62
    William   60
Whitlow, Redford   36
Wilbourn, Lewis   8
Wilkinson, Jesse   33
Williams, Drury   52
    Elizabeth   18
    James   66, 107
    John, 31, 106, 107,
            108

Williams, John M.   18
    Joseph   106
    Philip   1
    Powell   106
    Samuel   107
    Sol^n   71
    Solomon   1
    Thomas   36
    William   27, 35, 62
            86
    Zacharias   89
Willis, Bartlett   23
    Ellender   16, 102
    Ellin^r   82
    John   92, 97, 99
    Pleasant   82
    Salley   23
    Sarah   68
    William   16, 88, 98
            102, 108
Wills, Jesse   4
    Lawrence   80
Windle, Elizabeth   72
    Jane   72
Winfield, Mary   105
Winfrey, Hill   14
Wingfield, Fanny   4
    Francis   87
    Nancy   105
    Robert   84
Winn, Philip P.   25
Witt, Benjamin   59, 108
    J.   59, 63, 107
    Jesse   13, 70
    Mary   70
Wood, Christopher   19
    H.   6, 46, 80, 85
            94
    Henry   1, 17, 29, 62
            84, 93
    Lucy   29, 110
    Martha   9, 105
    Valentine 12, 41, 54
        55, 62, 76, 80
        84, 88, 99
Woodall, Shadrach   14
Woodram, Caty   77
Woodson, Benjamin   48
    Bouth   108
    Dorothea   110
    Drury   109
    E.   19
    Elizabeth   11
    Isham   76, 81, 90

148

Woodson, Isham R.   14
  J.   100
  Jacob   67, 75, 109
      111
  Jo.   7, 18, 36, 57
  John   3, 25, 45, 64
     80, 81, 86, 88
     90, 96, 99,102
    110
  Col. John   109
  John, Gent.   76
  John, Jr.   54
  John L.   82
  John S.   64
  Joseph 27, 28, 45, 50
    64, 76, 77, 81
    82, 91, 109, 110
  Joseph, Jr. 50, 110
  Joseph, Junr 77, 82
  Josiah   14, 65, 76,
    81, 105, 109
  J. R.   3
  Mary   48
  Matthew 28, 65, 82
    99, 109, 110
  Milner 20, 47, 110
  Nancy   77
  Philip 55, 81, 110

Woodson, Philip, Jr. 29
  Polly   42
  Richard A.   109
  Robert   27, 87
  Robert H.   55
  Sally   42
  Samuel 29, 55, 93
  Stephen 10, 67, 99
    110
  Susanna   26
  Tarlton   110
  Tarlton, Junr 109
  Thomas 8, 10, 82
  William   108
  W. N.   74
Woodward, Joshua 3, 14
    28, 51
  Samuel   56
  Susannah   56
Woolbanks, Salley 7
  Sarah   9

Y

Yarbrough, Fanney 111
  Thomas Griggs 111
Younger, Ann   31
  Samuel   75

* * * * * * * * * *

www.ingramcontent.com/pod-product-compliance
Lightning Source LLC
Chambersburg PA
CBHW061745270326
41928CB00011B/2383